VICTOR HERBERT

Victor Herbert in His Studio.
(Note the high desk at which he wrote.)

VICTOR HERBERT

The Biography of America's Greatest
Composer of Romantic Music

BY

JOSEPH KAYE

 BOOKS FOR LIBRARIES PRESS
FREEPORT, NEW YORK

First Published 1931
Reprinted 1970

780.924
K18v

69424

March, 1970

STANDARD BOOK NUMBER:
8369-5237-5

LIBRARY OF CONGRESS CATALOG CARD NUMBER:
74-109628

PRINTED IN THE UNITED STATES OF AMERICA

ILLUSTRATIONS

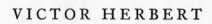
VICTOR HERBERT

VICTOR HERBERT

I

ONE autumn night in the eighties a young Irishman of twenty-seven, who had passed most of his life in Germany, took his place in the orchestra pit of the Metropolitan Opera House to play the cello. His name was Victor Herbert.

He had just arrived in New York, and from his obscure seat he looked around curiously at the mass of faces glowing weirdly in the vast, dim auditorium. He felt a symbolic force in the crowding immensity of the place, in the numerous dazzling points of light that leaped back from the precious stones on the hands and breasts of the women who sat in the two great curving tiers of boxes.

What future was he to have in this land?

The conductor emerged from the depths beneath the stage to his eminence on the podium. Applause rolled over the heads of the musicians below him. He raised his baton and the opera began.

Twenty-five years later, the same immigrant heard from the stage of the same theater the performance of an opera he himself had written. Similar rolls of applause came from the audience, but this time not to pass over his head in the pit. The acclaim was for him, a tribute to his artistry.

Thus, in the romantic fashion, may be outlined the beginning and the climax of the career of the most popular composer of light opera to be developed in the American theatre. And of one of the most beloved figures who ever made the rounds of Broadway.

"Dear old Victor!" spoken with affectionate, wistful recollection, sums up the sentiment of those who knew him. It is a recollection that seems more enduring than the seven-year-old lump of stone that seals his tomb in New York's Woodlawn Cemetery.

.   .   .   .

While the greatest wish of Herbert's life was to be known as a composer of grand opera, and he did write and see produced two such works, that desire was akin to the craving which inspires a comedian to dream of "Hamlet." His sphere was the operetta, and he will always be remembered by his legacy of captivating melodies.

His character was in true accord with the spirit of his major works. He was happy, deep-laughing, witty, appreciative of both cabbage and caviar, a good friend, a Rabelaisian story-teller. He was one of the last survivors of the city's real Bohemia, a member of Jimmy Huneker's circle, and a man who ardently loved the good things of life and worked with zest to earn them.

Apart from his music, Herbert had two great interests in life: good living and the cause of Irish independence. When he died he weighed about two hundred and fifty pounds, and it would not be an extravagance to say that he had eaten himself to death. He loved food and drink and could go into rhapsodic flights over a dish. But he was not a gourmand. Eating and drinking to him were not only to fill the stomach but for voluptuous enjoyment. He could talk for a week about a keg of Pilsener, and whenever he played a lengthy engagement in a theatre or park an ice box was always installed in his dressing room for liquors.

Prohibition threw him into a fury of revolt. "Mad enough to kill people!" his friends reported. He said that if it were not for the ties his children had made in this country he would ship back to Germany. Prohition! His heavy, cheery face was darkened by scowls when the subject came up. What a law! *Gott in himmel*, what a law!

He was well-proportioned, despite his size, and handsome and imposing. The moment he stepped into a room, those present knew a celebrity was among them. He was one of the few men in the American theatre to whom all Broadway deferred. Never was he "only the author." Broadway recognized him as a man of great talent, particularly as one who "knew his business." That meant he was no one-fingered melodist, but wrote his own piano parts and made his own orchestrations. A marvelous achievement for a Broadway musician!

He became accustomed to obsequious attention.

[3]

When he would come to a rehearsal conducted by Ned
Wayburn—then the director for Ziegfeld—the pro-
cedure was for Wayburn, as soon as he caught sight of
Herbert's tall, bulky, correctly-clad figure (he generally wore formal clothes in the afternoon), to turn to
his company and say:

"Mr. Herbert—everybody!"

The "everybody" was a signal for all to rise and
applaud. Herbert would smile and nod courteously
to the bloomered girls and shirt-sleeved men, carefully
raise his coat-tails and sit down at the piano. Wayburn
never kept him waiting. Whatever part of the show
had been in rehearsal was postponed and the numbers
requiring Herbert commenced forthwith. There was
tremendous respect for this man who "knew his business."

.   .   .   .

With all his liking for dignified bearing he could
easily relax, especially before a bottle of whisky or beer
and in the company of friends. In that congenial mood
he loved to dispense stories that, while not for the
family fireside, were good enough to be included in
a classic anthology.

For example, the story he told to the brothers of a
Pennsylvania monastery where he visited with his band
at the request of one of his musicians who had a brother
in the institution. There was a pious man, he said, who,
after being confessed by his old priest, returned to
admit that he had failed to include one sin in his re-

cital. After a long hesitation and mumblings that he feared his transgression was too great for forgiveness, he revealed that he had yielded to the sin of the flesh in a perverse manner.

The old priest was horrified. Positively there could be no absolution for such an abomination! The pentinent sorrowfully went away and, after wandering about for some time, decided to call on another priest. This time he was received by a young man, and, to his great delight, absolution was readily granted.

"But Father So-and-so (naming the other priest) told me I could never be forgiven," the man said, to which the young cleric responded:

"Oh, well, what does he know of such things!"

.   .   .   .

Herbert was a placid man, but when aroused he was capable of projecting a lurid flow of language. Usually these outbursts came in connection with his music. At rehearsals he was a tyrant, and so keen was his ear that if the second fiddlers played a G flat instead of an A, he would know it. So would the fiddler. But his men did not mind his verbal lashings. They knew he was a master of his art and were glad to please him. In return he was very generous to them, and notoriously easy for "touches."

Whenever his stalwart figure appeared on Broadway a bandsman would be sure to pop up from somewhere with a melancholy story. There was a time when Herbert would stop and patiently listen to the affecting details, but later he developed the more expeditious system of stuffing his pockets with bills of substantial denominations and when a musician with the unmistakable intent greeted him on Broadway he would nod a pleasant response, stick his fingers into a pocket, pass a bill to the man and be on his way almost without halting.

At the end of each season it used to be a formality with him to ask his men if he owed them money. (He often borrowed small amounts from them when he ran short.) Usually there were some men who spoke up. It was too tempting a chance for an easy five or ten dollars. Herbert never questioned such claims.

"Certainly, my boy, certainly," he would reply, and peel off a bill.

.   .   .   .

He loved flattery and expanded beatifically when, in passing through the streets of a small town where he was booked for a concert, some urchin would greet him with "Hello, there, Victor!" But he hated bunk and could detect the false note at once and be on his guard.

Pomp appealed to him enormously. He clothed himself with the best garments money could buy. He drove about town in a magnificent car. On the lake near his summer home in the Adirondacks he used the fastest speedboat he could get. He was careless with money and found it easy to spend like a prince. But he felt like one.

He was an indefatigable worker, and so prolific that

[6]

he could write two scores at the same time, walking from one to the other as they were spread out on a large table. He composed as other musicians do copying, the melodies literally flowing from his mind. He was also so expert at instrumentation that, when pressed for time, he wrote each individual part without bothering first to complete the score.

In spite of a good education in Germany Herbert's conversations usually were limited to shop. Or when he did not talk of music or the stage he reminisced. Topical events had little interest for him.

．　．　．　．　．　．　．

He was a true minstrel, this Victor Herbert, a singer of gay and charming songs and the liver of a genial life. And, like a good minstrel, if trouble came, rarely did any one know it but himself. He was fortunate in being appreciated almost at his full worth during his lifetime. But if a production were received indifferently he would not waste time brooding over it. Not that he did not vigorously resent the failure of any piece he believed should have been a success.

Once a friend was deploring that "The Madcap Duchess" had received such a poor reception. Herbert had but one comment to make for that: "It was too good for the bastards."

II

VICTOR HERBERT was born in Dublin, Ireland, on February 1, 1859. His father, Edward Herbert, a lawyer, died in Paris about two years later. Herbert never spoke much of him, and there is so little known of his life that he passes out of the composer's record without more than a bare mention.

But his mother brings us to attention. She was Fanny Lover, the daughter of Samuel Lover who, as it is perhaps necessary to say in this age of forgotten heroes, was a famous Irish man-of-all-arts.

Whether heredity played any part in Herbert's life is, of course, a matter of theory. But if artistic heredity can be considered a potent factor in a career, then Herbert received his talent directly from his grandfather.

Samuel Lover is remembered chiefly to-day as the author of two novels, "Rory O'More," and "Handy Andy." But these books were only a small part of his accomplishments. He was a painter, a poet, a songwriter, a singer, a dramatist, a humorist, a grand opera and comic opera librettist, a musician, actor and one-man entertainer. He was, too, an ardent Irish patriot and gave freely of his time and talent to the cause of Irish nationalism.

Though Herbert and his grandfather were opposites physically, Lover being small and frail, both men had somewhat similar temperaments. Lover, like Herbert, was gay, genial, social, warm-hearted, and of course always ready for a good story.

Almost equally with his artistic talents Herbert inherited his grandfather's patriotism.

In his youth, Lover saw terrible things. They were impressed forever on his mind and heart. He was born (also in Dublin, in 1797, and also on a February day) into a period of Irish insurrections. It was soon after his birth that rebellion broke out, and when he was only six, Robert Emmett shot his bolt.

"What tales were current then," he wrote, in describing his early life, "of hangings, floggings and imprisonment; of victims who were subjected to the torture of the pitch-cap, of citizens and others grossly insulted by the soldiery, and domiciliary visits made in the most savage and repugnant manner. How often also were heard the drums beating in the streets and the tramp of soldiers who were called out to search for arms in all directions. This I witnessed as a child."

Lover lived at that time near Marlborough Green and the building in which John Claudius Beresford, zealous representative of the government in crushing revolts, put the prisoners through an inquisition. Beresford's methods were so much in the manner of the old days in Spain that a party of Irishmen who still retained their sense of humor once stole a laundress' sign marked "Mangling done here," and hung it over the gate of the official's headquarters.

On his way to school young Lover passed this place

and its fresh history made him shudder. He was personally to experience a vicious episode of that time. The citizens of Dublin were ordered to billet the soldiers or give each man a shilling, the price of a bed elsewhere.

One afternoon a soldier and a drummer boy appeared at the Lover house for accommodations. They refused the two shillings which Mrs. Lover offered and became nasty. Mr. Lover, a stockbroker, was not yet home from his office, and his wife, clutching little Sam, ran out to the streets where Lover later found her, trembling and almost speechless. He ran into the house to protest. The soldier drew his bayonet and there might have been bloodshed had not an official from the billet office arrived in answer to a hurry call, and was fair enough to put the soldiers out and apologize to the Lovers for their conduct.

Samuel Lover later said of this incident: "What a scene was this for a delicate child to witness, one who was more than usually susceptible to terrifying impressions. Here was an English soldier outraging an Irish Protestant home. What other feelings could it awaken than that of aversion to a redcoat? In such a mental soil as mine is it a wonder that the seeds of patriotism took root and sprang up quickly? Every word I heard after that, of English oppression and Irish wrong, I eagerly caught and well remembered, till, in my sixteenth year, I had become as stanch an asserter of national rights as ever trod my native soil."

Though Lover spent much of his time in England

and his artistic activities calmed to some extent his pro-Irish sentiments, he was always the nationalist. Those feelings were completely absorbed by his grandson, at first through personal contact in early youth, and later through the admiration he felt for his distinguished relative.

For Victor Herbert's background it is also significant to note that song-writing was among Lover's earliest accomplishments. After rejecting his father's plans to make him a good stockbroker, and leaving home because the senior Lover had smashed a puppet theatre the boy had constructed (hated evidence of stage ambition), he first made a profession of painting, beginning with marine pictures and miniature portraits.

But when he was twenty-one, a banquet was given to Thomas Moore which was to have an important result for him. Receiving a ticket for the event from a friend, he was so overjoyed at the prospect of sitting at the same table with the poet that he composed a song eulogizing him. During the banquet the arrangers of the program discovered they had forgotten to prepare a lyric tribute to their guest of honor. Word was brought to the chairman that the youngster, Sam Lover, had just such a composition in his pocket, and was anxious to sing.

"Tell him to get ready," said the chairman, and shortly after the excited youth was called upon.

The tributory song, though delivered through a fog of stage-fright, pleased the assemblage and flattered Moore. The great man asked to be introduced to the singer, and the incident brought about a close friendship between the two men.

Victor Herbert was known to have an extraordinary memory for music. He could recall, if he could not always name, practically every melody he had ever heard. Lover had a similar trait. It showed itself to advantage in connection with a miniature he painted of Paganini, the monarch of all violinists.

Paganini, who had a most devilish appearance, being long, gaunt, wan, eagle-beaked and topped by a mass of wild, black hair, visited Dublin in 1832. Lover was eager to paint this unusual personality. The violinist consented to the portrait, but during the sittings he seemed dull. Lover tried to stimulate him into some animation. The following is the conversation reported to have taken place:

"I liked very much the little *capriccio motivo* from one of your concertos," Lover remarked, and then hummed the tune. Paganini looked surprised.

"You have been in Strassburg?" he asked.

"Never."

"Then how did you hear that air?"

"I heard you play it."

"No—if you were not in Strassburg."

"Yes—in London."

"That concerto I composed for my first appearance in Strassburg and I never played it in London."

"Pardon me," Lover gently insisted, elated at having struck a spark, "you did—at the opera house."

"I don't remember."

"It was the night you played an obligato accompaniment to Pasta."

"Ah, Pasta!" Paganini recalled with rapture the performance of the celebrated diva. "Yes, how magnificently she sang that night."

"And how you played!" Lover said, with a fine sense of timing.

Paganini accepted the compliment with a shrug that inferred carelessness but meant gratification.

"But the *motivo!* Yes—I did play it at the time, but only that once in London. You must be a musician! It is not an easy air to remember."

"It was encored, Signor," explained Lover, "and so I heard it twice."

"Ah, so. But still I say it is not easy to remember except by a musician."

And from this point on Paganini became so vivid a subject that Lover made the best miniature of his career. It was shown a year later at the Royal Academy in London and brought the artist, till then unknown in England, a reputation.

Herbert's grandmother also gave him an artistic heritage. She was a Miss Berrel, the daughter of a Dublin architect, a man described by near contemporaries as having "talent and refinement." She was a Catholic, and Lover a Protestant, but they agreed to avoid controversial topics arising from their faiths, an agreement easy for Lover to keep because of their common nationalism and his cultural interests. Through their union Herbert was part Catholic, though insofar as he considered religion at all he was known as a Protestant.

Lover married Miss Berrel in 1827, when he was thirty, and thereafter his home became a gathering place for Irish intelligentsia.

It was during this period that Lover joined the Dublin club which accounted in rather a large measure for Herbert's German connection. This was the *"Burschenshaft,"* founded by another Irish novelist, Charles Lever, to perpetuate in his own country the memories of his student days in Germany. Lover was appointed minstrel to the club, and his duty was to furnish poetry and songs on state occasions.

This club must have aroused Lover's interest in Germany, and probably an affectionate regard for its educational institutions and social life, for it was he who later suggested to his daughter that she take Victor to Germany for his schooling. And when Mrs. Herbert followed this suggestion she laid the foundation for her son's career.

Soon after painting the Paganini miniature, Lover went to London to live. He felt that his talents could better expand in that capital. From then on England was his home and the place where he created his most important works.

Strange how the careers of Herbert and Lover parallel even in their choice of residence. Though Herbert was intensely an Irishman he never lived in Ireland, except for the few years of his babyhood, and never felt a strong desire to return there except for a holiday. Lover lived his earlier life in his native country, but once having left it he preferred to be the expatriated nationalist.

In London, Lover became popular with the literary, art and social sets. He was known mainly as a painter and composer of songs. Later he took to writing novels and pieces for the theater.

He provided the celebrated musical comedy actress, Madame Vestris, with songs and an operetta, "The Greek Boy," composing the music as well as the words. His dramatized version of his own "Rory O'More" ran for a hundred nights at the Adelphi Theater, with Tyrone Power in the lead. He even ventured into burlesque grand opera, composing "Il Paddy Whack in Italia," which his friend and fellow Dubliner, Michael William Balfe, produced in London. Balfe was the composer of that most famous of all English operas, "The Bohemian Girl," but he was also a manager of musical enterprises. Lover wrote two grand opera libretti for Balfe which, however, was never produced.

In London, Lover was a happy, busy man. An American contemporary writer, in an article published in the *Boston Atlas*, gave this picture of him:

"But who is this lively little gentleman whom everybody is shaking hands with, and shakes hands with everybody in return? He is here, there and everywhere, chattering away delightfully, it would seem, and dispensing smiles and arch looks in profusion. How his black eyes twinkle and what fun there is in his face! He seems brimful and running over with good humor and looks as if care could never touch him.

[15]

"And listen to that Milesian brogue! Reader, perhaps you have never heard an educated Irishman talk? Well, if so, you have lost a treat, for nothing in this world is more delightful, except perhaps the soft, mellifluous, tripping-over-the-tongue tattle of a pretty, well-informed daughter of the Emerald Isle. That natty, dear duck of a man, as the ladies say, is a universal favorite. He is at once poet, painter, musician and novelist. He writes songs, sets them to music, illustrates them with his pencil, and then sings them as no one else can.

"Hurrah! We have Rory O'More amongst us. Sam Lover, I beg to introduce you to the American public. Mr. Public—the author of the 'Tale of the Gridiron', and, I assure you, one of the most accomplished and really elegant men you will ever have the good fortune to know."

This sketch of Lover, except for the multiplicity of accomplishments and physical appearance, could be that of Victor Herbert himself. Brimful of humor! Never a careworn face! That slight and ingratiating brogue! The favorite everywhere! That was Herbert. That is the picture that all Herbert's friends carry with them. Were it not that Victor Herbert possessed a true genius for his art and was inherently a natural man, one could theorize that he deliberately modelled himself after his grandfather.

.   .   .   .

In 1846, Lover had to pay out a large sum of money for a friend whose credit he had endorsed. To rehabilitate his finances he decided to go to America. His plan was to give a series of Irish monologues interspersed with songs, to be known as "Irish Evenings." At the same time he intended to paint landscapes of the new world.

Through introductions to Hawthorne and N. P. Willis, he was made warmly welcome when he arrived in New York. Thus he added another link between himself and Herbert, for the United States was to be a familiar topic of conversation in Lover's home in the future.

His first entertainment took place on September 28, of that year, at the Stuyvesant Institute. Tickets were a dollar. The *New York Herald* thus reported the event:

"On the occasion of Mr. Lover's first appearance the Stuyvesant Institute was crowded last evening to the utmost capacity with the beauty and fashion of the city, and numbers were unable to obtain admission.

"At eight o'clock, Mr. Lover made his bow to the audience and was received in a most cordial and flattering manner. It would be difficult to describe the nature of the entertainment so as to do it justice. We will content ourselves with saying that it was a flow of polished witticisms, puns, songs, jokes and recitations, combined with touches of deep pathos, delivered in such a felicitous style that the audience was at one moment completely beside themselves with merriment and another almost melted into tears.

"All the songs were of his own composition and

[17]

indeed, all new to this country except two or three. The 'Widow Machree', 'The Low-Backed Car', 'Rory O'More', and others created a perfect storm of laughter and applause.

"The gem of the evening was the recitation of a poem descriptive of an incident in the so-called rebellion of 1798. We will not attempt to describe it, for it must be heard to be appreciated. It is in a vein of true, hearty, genuine Irish feeling, that proves the author to be a whole-souled Irishman. It thrilled the audience in such a way that the applause at the end was continuous for several minutes. The story of the Gridiron was a rich treat, lighted up by the inimitable drollery which marked its recital.

". . . Mr. Lover has achieved a triumph of no ordinary magnitude. The élite of the city have turned out en masse to welcome him to our shores and his later entertainments will doubtless be just as crowded as that of last evening."

Altogether, Lover's visit to America was a success, his entertainments being well received wherever he went, though he did say that in the New England States the restrained audiences gave him a feeling of being a "voyager among icebergs." He traveled West and South and into Canada, painted a great deal, collected material for a book, and wrote his daughters enthusiastic descriptions of the country.

He remained in America nearly two years. During this time his wife, an invalid when he left her, died. He, however, kept on with his tour. By the time he was ready to leave, he had so firmly established his popularity that a New England fellow-traveler, in urging him to remain in the United States, thought he voiced the feelings of Americans by saying:

"Sir, you are admired and respected in this country, and you may rely on it, if you die here, we should give you a beautiful monument."

But it was his grandson who was to continue his popularity in America. It was his grandson who was to be given the monument promised Samuel Lover.

.   .   .   .

Returning home, Lover utilized his American experiences by giving American-Irish evenings. He toured successfully for two years.

It was about this time that his younger daughter, Fanny, married Edward Herbert. Not long after, his elder daughter died of tuberculosis. He could not endure being alone, and, in 1852, at the age of fifty-five, Samuel Lover married Miss Mary Waudby. She was to be the grandmother Victor Herbert knew.

Lover settled down to write and paint. He lived quietly in several country places, the last being Sevenoaks, on the outskirts of London. It was there that Fanny Herbert, when she became a widow, brought little Victor. And it was there that the career of the composer began.

From the day he stepped into his grandfather's home, the influence of Samuel Lover began to assert itself over young Herbert. The Irishman in him was carefully fostered, not only by Lover, but by the many Irish nationalists who visited Lover despite the fact that he was the recipient of a pension from Queen Victoria.

And as to music, Victor was to hear it daily, in all forms. His grandfather's guests were skilled musicians, and his mother was a competent pianiste. He heard many Irish folksongs, some of them crooned over his bed by his mother.

In Sevenoaks, too, old Mr. Lover would take Victor on his knees and tell him of all the wonders of America; of the strange city of New York, of the elemental magnificence of Niagara Falls, of the funny stories he had been told.

When Victor reached the age at which his formal education was to begin, Lover advised his daughter to take the boy to Germany. There, he thought, the educational facilities were better and cheaper than in England. It may also have been in the grandfather's mind that if young Victor's formative years were passed abroad the danger of his becoming Anglicized would be lessened.

Mrs. Herbert agreed with her father. She packed two portable baths with her luggage and she and Victor set off for culture.

The Continentals on their itinerary were somewhat flabbergasted by the English lady who erected her tubs and requested hot water and soap. But Mrs. Herbert smiled with tolerant independence, and, so traveling, they came to the south of Germany, and settled at Langenargen, on Lake Constance.

Here Mrs. Herbert made the acquaintance of a German physician, Dr. Carl Schmidt, whom she married; then the family moved to Stuttgart, where Victor's education was begun at the *Humanistisches Gymnasium*.

Herbert later in life spoke as little of his stepfather as he did of his own father. He used to become very angry when it was intimated that he was a German.

"I am a hundred per cent Irish!" he protested indignantly.

And yet there is a possibility that Herbert was half-German by birth. His father may have been a German. The name, Herbert, is used by Germans, and there were even two German composers of the same name contemporary with Herbert. Victor Herbert was so thoroughly the Teuton in appearance and habits that such a supposition may well be entertained.

The family plans for Victor at this time were not to make him a musician, but a doctor. The influence of Lover and the old environment had receded a little with the new German alliance, and the mother, as mothers usually are in such circumstances, was more inclined to agree with the opinions of her husband. Here, too, there is a parallel between the careers of Herbert and Lover, who, it will be recalled, also was not intended for an artistic profession.

In the correspondence of Lover available for examination there is a mention of his daughter and her German husband. This is in a letter written to his friend, Andrew J. Symington, dated April 29, 1866, from the Isle of Wight:

"MY DEAR MR. SYMINGTON—For the last week or ten days a 'change has come over the spirit' of the spring and bitterly cold easterly winds have been nipping us and making us doubt if we can venture out of this place of defense, where we have kept garrison during the past months, as soon as we could desire, for we want to get into Germany before the hot weather sets in. You must know I have a daughter, the wife of a German physician, living in Germany, (South), not very far from the Swiss Alps, and to her are Mrs. Lover and myself going on a visit. I think it will be well to take advantage of my amended health for the purpose of traveling at this particular time, for, at my age, a re-currence of disease, such as I have recovered from, might render me quite incapable of going so far; and I wish to see my dear child in her own home *once* again, at all events, before I am called from this scene of our trial. . . ."

Lover did not realize this wish. His health, which had been bad for a few years, prevented him from leaving England. He died on the sixth of July, 1868, in his seventy-second year, at St. Helier's, Jersey.

III

In Stuttgart, Victor Herbert began his studies in the college happily, not the least troubled by musical urges. It had been more or less settled that he should follow his stepfather's profession and the boy seemed satisfied.

His mother, like the cultured lady of her class, wanted Victor to know at least one musical instrument and begged him to learn to play the cello. In the Lover home, the noted cellist, Alfredo Carlo Piatti, had often been a visitor, and his performance so impressed Victor's mother that she longed to have her son sit behind the big fiddle and draw the same mellow, sentimental notes from it.

But Victor was too busy for music. He wanted to shine in his class, and what with games and schoolboy pranks, music would waste too much of his time.

He might eventually have obtained a doctor's degree and discovered his mistake later had it not been that, in preparing for a festival, the school band discovered it was short a flutist. A survey was made of available prospects, and Herbert was chosen to fill the gap. He was given orders to master the piccolo part of Donizetti's overture to "The Daughter of the Regiment," and to do it in two weeks.

With the diligence that later was one of his greatest characteristics, Victor got to work. His mother was vexed when she heard to what musical study her boy had attached himself. Of all instruments! A big, strapping boy blowing through a tiny tube! If he wanted music, why not the cello? Such a noble instrument!

But Victor swept away her objections with the brief reminder that he had orders. Regretfully, his mother bought him a piccolo.

Followed a nightmare of hideous sounds to torture the poor lady. She could not stand the shrill pipings of the piccolo.

"But, Victor, please, the cello—so much nicer—"

Not the least effect. The boy blew and panted and kept it up for hours a day. Within the given time, he proudly appeared for rehearsal and stumbled through his part correctly. On the festive occasion the overture came off nicely and the piccolo kept time and tune.

That was Victor Herbert's start in music. Not long after he made the acquaintance of a boy who played the violin well and as their acquaintance increased the other boy joined Mrs. Herbert in derogatory remarks about a piccolo player. This time Victor was inclined to listen. Besides, he liked his friend's violin playing. He told his mother she could get him a cello.

"Up to that time," Herbert was reported as saying in an interview published in the *Christian Science Monitor* in 1921, "I had been one of the first five in my class of fifty, but from the time I began the study of the cello, I took a drop in my work at the *Gymnasium*. Soon after there were financial troubles and while

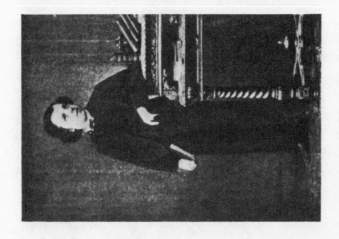

Herbert at School in Germany.

Herbert as a Concert Cellist.

By Boardman Robinson.

Victor Herbert, Composer and Conductor, at the Head of His Profession in America.

Caricature of Victor Herbert by Boardman Robinson.

my mother did not wish me to become a professional musician, she was told that I had a great deal of talent, and through the influence of the father of my violinist friend, I became the only pupil of Professor Cossman, of Baden-Baden. Cossman wrote a great deal for the instrument and was one of the best concert cellists of his day."

The financial troubles mentioned were brought about by expensive litigation over Samuel Lover's estate. Evidently Dr. Schmidt was not doing too well, either, or despite the litigation Herbert would not have been withdrawn from college, a necessity that must have hurt Mrs. Herbert very much.

In Baden-Baden, then a concentration place of the famous and wealthy, Mrs. Cossman kept a shop where she sold old laces. She was visited by such men as Von Bulow and Rubinstein, and so Herbert had the privilege of absorbing from these geniuses some of their spirit.

"I spent a year and a quarter in Professor Cossman's household," Herbert related in the same interview. "I had exceptional advantages. My lessons were no fifteen-minute affairs and then away at something else. I was under the constant eye of my master, and I could not help making rapid progress."

His progress was not only rapid but almost phenomenal, for soon he was sufficiently the expert to be employed by orchestras. All his retarded talent seemed to rush to the surface at the first opportunity and blossom into maturity in less time than it takes the ordinary musician to gain an elementary proficiency. His age when he began with Cossman was about sixteen.

Contrary to this record of Herbert's first musical studies, supported by statements made by Herbert himself, is the information given by Dr. Emanuel Baruch, the Herbert family physician and an old friend of the composer. According to Dr. Baruch, Herbert studied with a Professor Casbisius, a teacher of cello at the Stuttgart Conservatory, and with Emmanuel Faisst, professor of theory and composition. Possibly he started with Casbisius and then went to Cossman.

One of the orchestras with which he played was conducted by Eduard Strauss, a brother of Johann, the great writer of waltzes. Of him, Herbert related this incident in an interview published in the *Musical Courier*:

"When I was solo cellist with Eduard Strauss it was the regular duty of an old chap who played at the first desk of the second violins to rosin the bow for Eduard; that is, to pretend to rosin the bow, for the great Johann himself was the only one of the family who was a real violinist.

"Eduard used to go through all the motions, but very little music did that bow produce, for the old chap had his instructions. One evening this man was sick. A young player new to the orchestra sat in his place. Eduard came out, bowed to the applause which greeted him, and then handed his violin to the new man for the usual stage business to be gone through.

"He was an earnest, conscientious young man, and

he certainly got more dramatic effect out of rosining the bow than his older colleague had. The overture finished, the new man handed the violin back to Eduard with the bow, for the first waltz was next on the program and, as was the custom with the Strausses, Eduard was to lead, playing the violin. He struck an attitude with the bow poised; he raised his head; he nodded, and he swept the bow across the strings with a picturesque gesture. But—the new young man had not been told! There was some very real rosin on that bow. The introduction to that waltz was supposed to begin in the softest of pianissimos, and Eduard's unexpected, raucous scraping sent both orchestra and audience into roars of laughter."

Herbert said to friends that he played under many celebrated musicians in those days: under Liszt, Brahms, Rubinstein, Saint-Saëns and Delibes, all presumably guest conductors. He particularly remembered when Delibes, the French composer best known by his ballets, came to Vienna and was delighted by the Viennese turn that the orchestra with which Herbert played gave to his "Sylvia" music. This was a fond remembrance with Herbert, and he used it as an illustration of the difficulty of transferring to paper certain rhythms. The "Habanera" from "Carmen," for example, he said, would not have the same effect if played as written. It was all in the interpretation. He liked to add that Edwin Booth made himself famous by his rendition of just six words: "To be or not to be . . ."

After wandering about the Continent, sometimes as

a solo player with concert parties, and usually as a leading cellist with orchestras, the young musician returned to Stuttgart and joined the orchestra of the Court Opera as first cellist.

Some time before, while playing in Dresden, Herbert walked into the theatre where he was engaged, sat down at the piano, and began to improvise. He had never studied the piano, but picked up enough to do what he wished at the keyboard.

As melodies and chords flowed from the piano into the musty old auditorium, another musician of the orchestra came in—also a cello player. He listened to Herbert, slipped over to his side and said, when the player lifted his hands gently into the air after having caressed the last note of a sentimental passage:

"You should compose."

Herbert had thought but vaguely of composition until then, and he doubted whether he had it in him. The older player assured him he had and urged him not to waste time but to begin. When Herbert settled in Stuttgart he remembered this advice and put himself under the care of Max Seyffrytz, the *Hochkappelmeister*, for tuition in composition.

Seyffrytz was a man who believed that experience is the best teacher. He gave Herbert a grounding in harmony, counterpoint and orchestration, but at the same time set him to arranging a book of old melodies for cello or orchestra. No sooner was this finished than he required him to write a suite in five movements for cello and orchestra. Herbert finished this composition shortly after, and it was good enough to be played in public.

All this work was done within four months after he began his studies with Seyffrytz—truly prodigious progress. A year later he completed a concerto for cello and orchestra which was performed by the Royal orchestra.

Herbert was very grateful to the old German musician who had influenced him to write music. He corresponded with him regularly, and sent him his best compositions published in the United States. After the successful production of "Mlle. Modiste", Herbert made a special phonographic recording of the score of the operetta as a gift for his old friend. It was the only such set of records made.

He remained about five years in Stuttgart, and established himself as a popular young man-about-town. He looked more German than British and he took to German life as naturally as a native. He spoke the language fluently, he liked his German friends, and was ecstatic over the food and the beer. With his good-fellowship, and his high skill as a musical entertainer, he was a welcome guest in any home.

Dr. Baruch declares that in those days Herbert could have had his pick of the wealthiest and most attractive girls of the city. But Victor Herbert was too fond of life to be tied down. He contented himself with the charming affairs for which Europe is famous, and found complementary pleasures in the beer gardens.

One of the few known persons still living in Germany who knew Herbert at that time, an uncle of Fritz Stahlberg, the New York violinist and conductor, wrote to his nephew:

". . . we (Herbert, he and other young bloods of Stuttgart) never had any money, were always hungry and still more thirsty."

As Herbert presumably received a fair salary as first cellist of the court orchestra, his mode of life may be judged from the fact that he was always broke. He afterwards told how he could not pay the laundress and washed his own underwear at night, hanging it outside his window to dry overnight.

Once he started writing, however, he put forth a constant stream of music in all forms, mostly songs and short instrumental pieces. Among his concert appearances in Stuttgart were those as a member of a string trio which later was expanded to a quartet.

His fellow-artists in the first group were Pruckner and Singer, and in the second Singer, Seyboth and Wein. The first concert took place on October 30, 1885, with a program of a trio by Beethoven, a sonata by Rubinstein and the first performance in Stuttgart of the Brahms trio, op. 87. The second concert, given by the quartet, consisted of the Haydn quartet in C minor, the Schubert quartet in A minor and another Stuttgart première of Brahms, of the quintet, op. 88.

The group was evidently experimenting and trying to establish a permanent organization, for its concerts were far apart. The third concert took place in the following year and Herbert was no longer a member.

There came to the Stuttgart opera a young singer named Therese Foerster who had previously sung in the Vienna Opera House. Fraulein Foerster was a statuesque, handsome girl who made an impression on the opera patrons as much by her appearance as by her voice. Herbert was similarly impressed. Or perhaps the new soprano was impressed by Herbert, as other women were. Details are missing.

At any rate, a romance sprung up. It was fostered by the fact that Fraulein Foerster needed coaching, and Herbert spent much time with her at the piano.

That was in 1886, when Herbert was twenty-seven.

In the spring, just before the close of the opera season, a young man arrived in Stuttgart named Walter Damrosch. His father, Dr. Leopold, the director of the Metropolitan Opera Company in New York, had recently died, and the precocious son had been sent to Europe to find voices for the German operas which were to be featured by the management.

Young Damrosch wanted to include Therese Foerster. Though her voice was not of the first quality, she was young and good-looking, two virtues hard to find in divas then, as now.

But while Fraulein Foerster was willing to go to America and was agreeable to Damrosch's terms, there was one consideration that stopped her. She was engaged to Herr Victor Herbert, the cellist of the orchestra, and would not think of leaving him.

Damrosch was a bit puzzled. But her career? New York was a city to which all European artists wished to go; a new country, new audiences, much money. Would she miss such an opportunity?

The young woman was not at all excited. Amerika might be all that the Herr Damrosch said, and the Metropolitan a magnificent place to sing, but she would not leave her Herr Victor Herbert.

Damrosch went to interview Herr Victor Herbert. He heard him play and returned to Fraulein Foerster. Would she go if Herr Victor Herbert went with her? Went with her as what? As first cellist of the Metropolitan.

Ah, ja! Certainly she would go. That would be a pleasure.

Herbert was quite willing. Both signed contracts to appear at the Metropolitan that fall and Herbert was elated to know that the chief conductor under whom he would play was the eminent Anton Seidl.

That summer the couple married, and soon after left for New York.

The voyage cut Herbert off from all his former connections. He was to enter into a new life, into a new career, although no one would have been more surprised than he to have been told that.

Strange what incidents deflect the entire course of an individual's life. If Herbert had not met Therese Foerster, and if Damrosch had not wanted to engage her, and she had not insisted that he take him with her, Victor Herbert might not have come to the United States, there to be inspired by the Bostonians to write comic opera, the work that gave him his place in musical history.

IV

VICTOR HERBERT's arrival in New York was completely under the auspices of his wife.

No one knew him. He was only a cello player earning sixty dollars a week. But she was one of the great singers imported from Europe, among whom was the one and only Lilli Lehman. He sat in the orchestra pit and his wife appeared in all the dazzling glory of the Queen of Sheba in Goldmark's opera of that name, which opened the season.

Whatever natural charms Mrs. Herbert-Foerster (as she was known professionally) possessed were considerably amplified by the occasion, which was very gala.

The Metropolitan Opera House was in the throes of reconstruction. Four years previously, a group of rich men, considering the old Academy of Music on Fourteenth Street beyond the pale of aristocratic theater-going, and being in addition restricted by the older set in box-holding, created the present abnormal edifice.

The designing of the new temple of music was entrusted to Cleveland Cady, an architect who never before had built a theater, and his conception of a good auditorium was one in which the balconies ran in deep horseshoe formation, with the result that those spectators trapped in long sides of the balconies had only partial glimpses of the stage. Their anger, from then till now, has been such that no music could or can assuage.

During the first season the Metropolitan was leased by the society owners to Henry K. Abbey, who, in one fall, winter and spring lost no less than $600,000. The catastrophe for poor Abbey was so great that a benefit was held for him at the end of the season for which even newspaper critics refused complimentary tickets. From which phenomenal happening the plight of the unfortunate impresario can be correctly estimated.

The enormous sum of $36,000 was realized, but Abbey was not present to find solace in this practical manifestation of sympathy. Disaster had piled upon him heavily. Even as the last preparations were being made on the afternoon of the benefit, Abbey's wife died in his arms.

As a pendant note, it might be said that the Abbey benefit brought in the greatest sum for a single indoor performance in this country until Morris Gest presented Eleonora Duse to New Yorkers, shortly before her death.

Conditions did not improve at the opera house in the next couple of years and finally, in a desperate effort to save the diamond horseshoe from decay, it was decided to try out German opera, especially the operas of Wagner, which were then beginning to attain popularity in Europe.

Dr. Leopold Damrosch was engaged as the first director of the new régime, and his first season, 1885, was very successful. Upon his death, his work was

[34]

assumed, in part, by his son, Walter, and the Metropolitan proprietors, as well as the operatic public, were anxious to see whether the young man was up to the task.

The 1886-7 season was Walter's second. A royal crowd of social and intellectual celebrities turned out for the opening. "The Queen of Sheba" was selected as the first offering because of its splendid fittings, and because, it may be suspected, Frau Herbert-Foerster was not yet afflicted with operatic chestitis.

The cast included Lilli Lehman as "Shulamith", and Marianne Brandt as "Astaroth." Anton Seidl, Wagner's pupil, conducted. Mrs. Herbert was in greater company than any other young Metropolitan debutante. But she was not a lady to get excited. She sang the part capably and got good notices the next morning. The *World* wrote:

"Frau Herbert-Foerster is a singer from the royal opera houses of Dresden and Stuttgart, and Mr. Stanton (the business director of the opera) may be congratulated on having secured an artist of exceptional ability. She has a fine stage presence, and a dramatic soprano voice of great beauty and power. She was in every way well-suited to the rôle allotted to her. Her rendering of the great dramatic scene opening the second act revealed many beauties not brought out last year, and the success gained by Frau Herbert-Foerster during the evening leads us to look forward with pleasure to her appearance in other great dramatic rôles during the season."

The *Times* also liked her and observed in that caustic tone which overtakes all commentators on opera when divas are discussed:

"The newcomer, Frau Herbert-Foerster, was received with favor. Her mezzo-soprano voice has both strength and resonance, and her comeliness, for the first time since 'The Queen of Sheba' was made known in this country, rendered Asad's infatuation comprehensible."

The audience admired her, and when she made her entrance there was that sudden murmur in the air that indicated a new personality had created an impression.

An interruption should be made here for the benefit of a lively piece written by one of Mr. Pulitzer's bright reporters, descriptive of the audience that foregathered on that glittering occasion forty-five years ago. The following is from the *World's* three-section review of the opening:

"During the performance absolute quiet obtained, even bursts of applause being withheld until the end of the scenes, but during the intermission buzzing was quite *en regle*. It was a trite tribute to youth and beauty that made the Gould box a target of every glass, as in it sat not only the Wall Street Mephistopheles, but his son and heir and bright-faced bride.

"'Which is Field?'

"'Is Jay Gould here?'

"'How well George looks!'

"'Quite pretty, isn't she?'

"'I wonder if Jim Bennet will drop in?'

" 'Whitelaw Reid has cut his hair!'

" 'D. O. Mills doesn't look a day older than he did twenty years ago.'

" 'See Uncle Dan Sickles; he's always on parade.'

" 'What in thunder is Blaine doing here?'

" 'The man with the sharp profile is Andrews, the oil man.'

" 'Morton looks well; I suppose he'll loom up in Washington.'

" 'I'd like to banish the woman who wears that hat.'

"And by the way, if Director Stanton cares for immortality he can easily secure it by enforcing common-sense rules of head-dressing. Scores of men who paid $8.00 for two seats last night saw very little of the stage and nothing of what passed in the way of action. Those hats, high and wide, must go. High hats bother no one, but wide hats, feathers and bands are an unmitigated nuisance and should be denied admittance.

"Socially, the first performance was a pronounced success. Artistically, what more could be desired?"

And in this final conclusion there is substantial praise for Herbert's wife, for it was somewhat of a notable feat to be in harmony with the distinguished artists with whom she sang.

It is odd that Lilli Lehman, in the story of her life which she wrote in 1913, made no mention whatever of Frau Herbert-Foerster, though she wrote of her other colleagues. Perhaps the new soprano's youthfulness may have been to blame, for Mme. Lehman, even in those days, when she was thirty-eight, was already a bulky woman.

She did record her impression of "The Queen of Sheba", as it was given the year before (with another singer as the Queen), and it is worth quoting here to show the magnificence amidst which Mrs. Herbert made her American début, as well as for an inelegant little incident which one might have thought beneath the dignity of the queenly Lilli.

" 'The Queen of Sheba' was brought out with a gorgeous mounting that cost $80,000. An immense army of supernumeraries, real black and brown slaves, with women and children, was at the command of the theater, and I envied them for their complexions, for I would have liked to have painted myself for Aïda just their color. When the children knelt and stood before King Solomon with their presents, a little stream meandered forth from the brown group of little ones, rippled serenely and certainly towards the prompter's box and there disappeared unobtrusively, but left its trace behind, to the delight of the audience."

During this season, Mrs. Herbert sang four rôles at the Metropolitan: "The Queen" in "The Queen of Sheba"; "Elsa" in "Lohengrin"; "Aïda" and "Irene" in Wagner's "Rienzi." But she never appeared there again.

Why Mrs. Herbert, after so promising a start, left the Metropolitan is a minor musical mystery. There are three different solutions. As each one directly concerns Victor Herbert, they are here detailed.

First is the version of Alice Nielsen, the dainty little soprano for whom Herbert wrote some of his best operettas. Miss Nielsen has a warm regard for the composer's wife. She believes it was Mrs. Herbert who persuaded the composer to select her for the leading rôle in "The Serenade," an opportunity which resulted in her first great success and in her association with Herbert.

Miss Nielsen was in the Herbert home one afternoon after he had established his reputation as a composer. The talk turned to the early days. As he was reminiscing, he put his arm affectionately around his wife, saying that he owed everything to her.

"After I wrote my first operetta," he said, "she left her career and gave herself to me. 'I can help you better at home than on the stage of the Metropolitan,' she told me."

This affecting little scene is upset, however, because Herbert wrote his first produced operetta in 1894, and Mrs. Herbert left the Metropolitan in 1887, seven years earlier. Herbert also wrote one operetta which was not produced, the date of which cannot be placed; but it is certain he did not begin writing for the theatre until a number of years after his arrival in this country. If nothing else, Mrs. Herbert's salary as a leading opera singer would have been a strong reason for her remaining with the Metropolitan.

Several persons who knew the Herberts in the early days say Mrs. Herbert gave up the opera because children came. This also may be disproved by the fact that a year after she left the Metropolitan she appeared with a German operatic troupe in the Thalia Theatre, on the Bowery.

Another reason was given by Dr. Emanuel Baruch, the family physician.

"Mrs. Herbert was a beautiful woman," he said, "and —well, how would any man feel if his wife was in a love scene with another man, even though it were on the stage? Herbert was a sensitive man and it troubled him. He was, in a way, jealous of her, and insisted on her leaving opera."

Dr. Baruch is quite convinced that jealousy was the reason. He points out that had Mrs. Herbert wished she could have had any number of admirers in Europe, and this knowledge preyed on Herbert's mind. But here again the flaws intrude. There seemed to be a perfect understanding between Herbert and his wife in those days; in fact, it was Mrs. Herbert who might have been touched with jealousy, for she was anxious to spend as much time with her husband during the performances as she could.

Franz Kaltenborn, the conductor, who was with the opera orchestra, says that Mrs. Herbert was always hovering about her husband. When she was on the stage they used to exchange smiling glances and frequently Mrs. Herbert sang passages directly for Victor, as he sat at his cello in the pit.

"I recall how concerned she was about his health," he said. "Herbert was fond of smoking big, black cigars and she thought they were bad for him. She made a

Mrs. Victor Herbert a Few Years
After Her Arrival in New York.

Victor Herbert, Mrs. Herbert and Their Children,
Ella and Clifford, at Camp Joyland, Lake Placid.

practice of getting at his coat and substituting light cigars. At the intermission or the end of the performance Herbert would discover the substitution and swear. But he used to submit with the manner of a boy yielding to his mother's better judgment."

Nor do any other of his friends think that he was ever jealous of his wife, or that he ever had reason to be.

Walter Damrosch, who might have known the facts, does not remember them. He has only a dim recollection that Mrs. Herbert left the Metropolitan of her own accord.

It is more than possible that Mrs. Herbert abandoned her career for quite another reason. It is likely that her husband did insist on her leaving, and that his motive was jealousy, as Dr. Baruch intimates. But not a sentimental jealousy.

Herbert was an extremely vain man. His very physical personality seemed to have been built to create vanity. He was tall, strongly built, handsome, imposing, vigorous and full of life. It was possible that his wife's prominence affected him. She was the opera queen, talked and written about; he was an obscure cellist. There was no balance to that.

He had a strong, if unspoken, feeling that of the two he should dominate. And as Mrs. Herbert loved her husband exceedingly, and was, by nature, a home person to whom the good management of a house and family was even more interesting than the creation of an operatic rôle, she could yield to him without too much aggravation.

That she appeared later with another opera company can be discounted, because the Thalia troupe was insignificant and meant little in the musical world. In fact, the Thalia engagement should be proof that love jealousy played no part with Herbert in her leaving the Metropolitan.

Though the Herberts' marriage originated in love, they were unhappily mated. Herbert was not a man of fixed interest where women were concerned, and he differed characteristically from Mrs. Herbert. He was never more happy than when in the midst of Metropolitan camaraderie and gayety; she was contented with her home. Herbert was a brilliant man-of-the-world with a driving force that kept him always on the go; she was of *hausfrau* sluggishness. Nor did she seem to have the dominating interest in music that a woman in her position would be supposed to have. She had the voice but not the temperament of a prima donna.

As Herbert rose in his work, his wife receded from the picture. Though his music was soon to be concerned wholly with the English theatre, she never could master even a working knowledge of the English language and had constantly to be corrected in such elementary phrases as "I can't come", which she twisted to, "I no come."

And the years were unkind to her. Within a short time after her marriage she grew stout, and by the time Herbert won his first stage success she must have weighed close to two hundred pounds. With this obesity came a sharp fading of her former handsomeness. In contrast, Herbert, though also grown stouter, retained, and even added to his cavalierly dash.

In time this contrast was the cause of sharp scenes. A friend who was an intimate of the couple in the nineties says that Herbert became very callous with his wife and called her *"dumme Therese."* In this friend's presence he flung ugly German epithets at her, and once he spoke to her in some such derogatory manner before the noted composer, Scharwenka.

Of his conduct outside of his home he was considerately careful. Sam Finkelstein, one of his orchestra players, with whom he was particularly friendly, tells this incident:

"When we were in Montreal for the out-of-town opening of 'The Singing Girl,' Herbert and I were sitting in the Windsor Hotel, drinking cocktails and talking. Herbert kept on swallowing one after another. I never knew another man who could drink so many, and without showing any effect. I could not possibly keep up with him, and he reproached me for being a weakling.

"A party of girls from the show came in. They were pretty girls, provokingly attractive. Victor looked at them and sighed.

" 'Can't go around with pretty girls any more,' he said.

" 'Why?' I asked, laughing.

" 'I'm becoming too well-known,' he replied. 'They'll point their fingers at me.' "

But later he became indifferent. Another of his associates, who knew him some years after, said that he frequently telephoned him to meet him at lunch.

"It was usually at the Cadillac, the Hofbrau, Maxine's (a restaurant at Thirty-eighth Street, between Sixth Avenue and Broadway, now with the ghosts). I would find Herbert there with a young woman, and I was soon to know that my rôle on such occasions was that of guardian of appearances.

"Often Herbert's companion was a tall, buxom, Germanic blonde, and I used to wonder at his taste. Our drinks were usually champagne."

Mrs. Herbert, too, became indifferent. She had her home and her family, and she was content with them.

She always loved her husband and was proud of his fame. She survived him only by a short time, and her friends said she grieved so much she died of a broken heart. To this Dr. Baruch remarked: "Of a broken heart—plus diabetes."

But whatever the manner of his life with Therese Foerster, Victor Herbert was an affectionate father. They had five children, of whom two survived. Ella Victoria, the eldest, is now Mrs. Robert Stevens Bartlett, living in New York. Clifford Victor is the son. One child, Maud, died early, and two babies were born dead.

Clifford was the favorite child of both Victor and

Mrs. Herbert. In her childhood Ella often complained bitterly: "They never scold Clifford."

But it turned out to be Ella who was to be closest to her father. In later life, when he was disappointed with how his affairs were managed by others, he turned all his business over to her. She proved herself an apt executive for her father.

Herbert took great delight in playing with his children when they were small. Miss Nielsen remembers the time he brought home a train for Clifford and rolled all over the carpet with it. Clifford found it hard to get at the toy, but he had great fun watching his father's antics.

Once, when he was playing with his band in a Jersey amusement park, Herbert took the children for a round of the amusement devices and was stuck on top of the Ferris wheel. His great, hearty laugh (which always made his stomach quake) could be heard above the blaring of the carrousel organs and carnival noises.

When Ella was about ten and Clifford eight, a strange whim seized Herbert to have his children baptized. He called up his lawyer, at that time Charles Lellman (since dead) who arranged with Mr. and Mrs. Louis Schmidt, the former a colleague of Herbert's, to act as godparents. The next day, at St. Agnes Episcopal Chapel, on West Ninety-sixth street, New York, the children were baptized.

It is interesting to see how Herbert's vanity extended even to the naming of his children. Both Ella and Clifford bear a second moniker, Victoria and Victor.

Neither of his children is musical. Clifford was made to take up the violin and was taught by Henry Burck, Herbert's concert master. Burck wanted to please Herbert, and after great effort, trained the boy to play, "The Low-Backed Car," Samuel Lover's famous song.

Herbert was delighted. But it was the only delight he ever got out of his son's musical ability.

Victor Herbert, the Wizard Behind the Music.

V

BEFORE Herbert wrote his first operetta he put in eight years of varied musical activities. He became the very synthesis of American initiative and energy. He adopted this country readily, and because there was, at that time, a Bohemia here which compared favorably with the Bohemias of European capitals, he found himself at home.

In his early days his mother came to visit him, a little old lady, bright and clever, who caused wonder by smoking cigars. Unlike her son, she preferred life across the ocean and soon returned to Germany.

At the Metropolitan, Herbert began to be noticed because of the keen interest he took in the general ensemble of the opera orchestra. He was, according to every estimation, a very fine cellist, one of the best of those resident in America. This and his all-round musicianship, which included an expert knowledge of the orchestra, drew the attention of Anton Seidl, the first conductor of the Metropolitan.

Seidl was probably the greatest Wagnerian conductor of his time, the favorite pupil of Richard Wagner and a commanding musical personality. He was immensely popular in New York, and his strong, sensitive face, emphasized by long, artistic hair, could be identified by most cab drivers.

Seidl began to use Herbert for many little tasks, and, as he accomplished these eagerly and competently, he later made him his assistant for the summer concerts he gave every year at Brighton Beach.

This was a notable recognition of the young man's talents and also, to some extent, of his ingratiating personality and his ability to get along with orchestral musicians.

At the Brighton Beach concerts—famous as the chief attraction of the once noted and smart seaside resort not far from Coney Island—Herbert was programmed as "Assistant Conductor," under Seidl's name. It was for these concerts that Seidl asked him to write the "American Fantasy," and this composition, as well as some other orchestral pieces belonging to Herbert's serious period, were performed with some frequency by this orchestra.

As the Metropolitan gave only three evening performances and one matinée a week its musicians had considerable time at their disposal. Many of them also played with the Philharmonic Society, which gave only six concerts the entire season. Herbert was among these, and was solo cellist, first under Theodore Thomas, and later, when Thomas went to Chicago to organize a symphony orchestra there, under Seidl.

Besides these diversified orchestral engagements, Herbert branched out as a concert artist and played at musicales, home gatherings, benefits and concerts. There were few activities in the cello line in which Herbert did not participate. He even went out with barnstorming concert parties at which condensed versions of operas were given. He was an excellent go-getter, and flourished immensely in the zestful atmosphere of the New World.

In those days he also taught his instrument at the National Conservatory, a free institution founded by Jeanette M. Thurber, where he had as colleagues some of the most celebrated musicians in the world. Antonin Dvorák was there, and as Antonin was a remarkable drinker, he and Victor Herbert must have found each other congenial company.

James Huneker was a member of the staff of the Conservatory, and to this master Bohemian was assigned the job of showing the other Bohemian around town when Dvorák arrived. Antonin started off the day with mass at a Bohemian church which Huneker searched out for him—with some disappointment—and then the guide ventured to suggest a taste of that American nectar called a cocktail.

Dvorák was agreeable and Huneker took him to a place called Goerwitz'. As the eminent composer seemed to swallow smoothly, Huneker escorted him to a second hazard and as this was also negotiated with surprising facility, he embarked on a tour of what he called the "great thirst belt of central New York."

Soon the future composer of the "New World Symphony" was inverting his nineteenth cocktail. Huneker, more of a beer drinker, had practically reached his limit, and inquired whether the master would not like something to eat. The master declined with something like surprise, and counter-suggested a trip to an East Side restaurant for a dessert of *slivovitch*, a valued European alcoholic concoction. Those who claim that Herbert could out-drink any man in the musical or theatrical professions either forgot, or did not know, of his colleague, Antonin Dvorák.

Amongst Herbert's enterprises was membership in the Schmidt-Herbert string quartet. It was organized by Louis Schmidt, a talented violinist and fellow-orchestral player. Schmidt came of a musical family, his father being organist of St. Marks-on-the-Bowery. The other players were Franz Kaltenborn, viola, and Henry Schmitt, second violin, both fine musicians.

The quartet started excellently. The critics gave its first concert, held on December 9, 1891, an almost enthusiastic reception, as this review from the *Sun* will indicate:

"A truly musical evening—musical in the best sense of the word, since every note and phrase of it was beautiful in conforming to the highest rules of art—was given to the audience assembled last night in Hardman Hall. Though the names of these four artists who make up the Schmidt-Herbert quartet are favorably enough known to assure the public that good work might be looked for from their hands, yet such brilliant and intelligent playing as they actually presented to their patrons was something in the nature of a revelation. The real facts were plainly apparent. In detail, these facts were, first, the possession by each man of an exceptional tone, the breadth and sonority being simply remarkable. This was due, of course, to the purely musical voice, free from noisy vibration, which was in each case drawn by the artist from an extraordinarily fine instrument. There was not a suspicion of that scraping, stringy sound so often the disfigurement and bane of chamber music. Next, the absolute military precision of attack with which the four began each sentence was noticeable. Lastly, the brisk energy, the intellectual clearness that stamped out each phrase distinctly, with a right and judicious meaning, formed the crowning grace and excellence. The audience was quick to appreciate the merit of what it heard and after the Schumann quartet was recalled by a burst of heavy and genuine applause."

There was the opportunity at that time for a distinguished string quartet to develop in New York. The city was the pioneer capital of music, and it was fast showing the characteristics which, within a quarter of a century, were to make it the most important city for music in the world.

But Herbert's vanity wrecked that quartet, and its disbandment broke Schmidt's heart.

Schmidt is now an old gentleman of seventy-five. He lives in a small apartment in Sunnyside, Long Island. He has a resentful story to tell of the quartet. The memory of its failure lives like a canker in his soul. It probably warped his life. Listening to his account, one marvels at the potency of what, to the world at large, must be a very insignificant event.

Four men once got together; and four men separated. But what this meant to one man! Schmidt saw in his successful quartet the fame and reward for which his heart had yearned when he had been a musician in an orchestra. One of thousands of players who remain in obscurity all their lives, that had been his great opportunity to leave the ranks. But just as the step was made—crash! All over, and forever.

Because Herbert had achieved a reputation as a cellist, Schmidt, although he led the quartet and was its business manager, shared the profits equally with Herbert, the other two men being on a salary basis. After a time, Herbert began to show signs of dissatisfaction. He was primarily irked by the fact that Schmidt's name came first in the organization's name and that, as the first violinist, he received the major share of attention from audiences and critics.

"Of any quartet," Schmidt comments bitterly, "the cello is the tail, but Herbert wanted to be the head."

Herbert became difficult to handle. He had to be consulted on engagements and refused to be bothered. At last Schmidt decided to bring matters out in the open.

"Friend Herbert," he said, "what's the trouble? I must know. I must know on which side my bread is buttered."

Friend Herbert showed a little embarrassment, but he said that whenever he was engaged to play at a concert alone he was paid seventy-five or a hundred dollars, but that the same people could engage the quartet for a hundred and fifty or two hundred dollars, and thus get him for half the price, or less. That was bad business, he insisted—unfair to his reputation. He thought they should discuss it with Henry Wolfson, the concert manager who got Herbert his solo engagements. Schmidt agreed.

Obviously, Herbert wanted to head the quartet himself.

"Who ever heard of a cellist leading a string quartet?" Schmidt demands in an outraged voice. "And didn't I organize it? Didn't I work to get the subscribers and the engagements? After we organized I decided to ask bankers and other rich people to subscribe to our concerts. I had never done such soliciting before. It was not a pleasant thing to do, and I didn't like it. But it was for the success of our quartet, and I said I would go, and that I would get the subscriptions, too!

"Herbert laughed at me. He thought I was too quiet for such a job. He said in German: 'You, with your kid gloves! You'll turn tail when you come to the door!' But I said, 'You'll see!'

"The next day I began. I worked hard, and despite my 'kid gloves' I managed to get a large number of subscriptions. I was very happy, and as soon as I was able I ran to see Herbert. I found him in the bar of the old Lenox Lyceum and showed him my list of subscribers.

"Now I ask you, what would most men have said if such a list had been brought them? What would any colleague, any ordinary, considerate man, say? Wouldn't he at least say: 'That is good!' But what did Herbert say? He just glanced carelessly through the list and remarked: 'The first day is always the easiest.' That was all. Nothing more."

That brusque remark of Herbert's seems graven on the old violinist's heart.

"And it was I who got all the engagements," he insists. "I did all the work. And I got high prices for us, too. Once I got an engagement at a private musicale given by the daughter of a well-known politician in Troy. They paid us two hundred dollars for the evening. A very high price. The highest price I had ever heard of for such an engagement."

Herbert and Wolfson then got together with Schmidt in Putsch's beer place in Madison Square Garden.

"Wolfson began talking," Schmidt says, "and he talked to me just as Herbert had talked. I didn't say anything until he was finished, and then I said: 'I don't know whether friend Herbert has told you all, but you ought to know exactly what I have done for the quartet.' And then I explained to him all the facts. Wolfson didn't have a word to say after that.

"Well, we parted and didn't come to any agreement. Herbert just let it go and we continued as before, but with the same difficulties for me. I had the hardest time to get him to coöperate. If I could at last corner him somewhere and tell him we had to give an answer, yes or no, about an engagement, he would say: 'Why bother me?' And yet he had to approve all engagements. I could not arrange them without his agreement.

"We went along like that until the next season, when

I was surprised to hear from some friends who told me they had seen a circular about the quartet which Wolfson had sent out, and that the name was the 'Herbert-Schmidt' quartet.

"Herbert was then playing with an orchestra at Saratoga Springs and I wrote him there, asking him why the name had been changed without my knowledge. Herbert sent me back a letter, and I wish I had kept it as a curiosity. Every other word was an oath."

The recollection of Victor Herbert's picturesque language can banish a little of Schmidt's bitterness.

"How he could swear!" he laughs.

"Well," the story continues, "Herbert finally told me it was Wolfson's fault and that as the circulars had already been sent, why not let the changed name remain for the season? What could I do? I didn't want more trouble. So I agreed. But when the same thing happened the next season, and Herbert didn't seem to care much, we broke up."

Schmidt has some further reflections on Victor Herbert.

"If you played up to Herbert right you could own him," he declares. "He was always attracted by the bright lights, and could never stand being second. Once we played at a function in a house in Washington Square. There were many notables there. I remember only General Horace Porter. I had composed for the occasion a little Spanish thing which I played solo on the violin and it went very well. I was applauded and some of them congratulated me. But did Herbert say a word to me? Not one!

"He loved doing the grand thing if others could see him. Once he went to a bazaar that was given for the benefit of an actor. He went through the place with his large smile. Then he stopped at a flower booth and bought a rose. In payment he counted out three hundred dollars.

"He had no patience with those he didn't like, and I had a lot of trouble with him whenever we played at some fashionable home where the ladies tried to treat him as a guest. There were, in those times, a number of amateur chamber music societies, composed only of women. These women sometimes engaged us to play for them and also with them. That is, Herbert and I would play with two of the members, or one of us would play with two or three of them. It was an awful ordeal, for the women generally were not only without much talent but often could not even play correctly. All we could do was to try to keep up with them and it was a job to watch when they would skip a measure. Herbert disliked these clubs, but they paid well, and they bridged the better engagements. We had to take them. What could we do? A new musical organization must struggle and suffer before it becomes established.

"But Herbert had no tact at all, and when the concert was over he wanted to run off at once. The ladies tried to entertain us, and usually had dainty refreshments which to Herbert were detestable.

"On one such occasion they had oysters, delicately prepared, and ice cream and cake. After the recital they gathered about us. Herbert glared at the table with the delicacies and then began tugging at my sleeve. As the women were talking to me, I could not answer him, and he tugged harder. Finally he said in German, in a voice those near us could not help hearing: 'Come on out of this God-damned place and let's get some beer.'

"Herbert's beer once caused me great embarrassment. I had arranged for a concert in Brookline, Massachusetts. We were going there from Boston, and as it was early, I left Herbert, Schmidt and Kaltenborn in a Boston hotel bar and went on to Brookline with an accompanist, for there were some solos to be played.

"The recital was to start at eight. At that hour, Herbert and the others had not arrived. The lady who had engaged us began to be worried, and so was I. A half hour passed, and another half hour, and still they had not arrived. I began to see our check disappearing, and the audience was becoming loudly impatient. Trying to kill time I said I would begin with my solos. Fortunately, our employer agreed, and it was only after I had finished that Herbert showed up with the others. He had been unwilling to leave the bar, and thought nothing of holding up a concert. But what upset me even more than that was his coming in without a word of apology."

In contrast to Herbert's usual generosity to his orchestral comrades, when some years later Schmidt was badly off and wrote to Herbert, who was then the conductor of the Pittsburgh Symphony Orchestra, he received no answer. Nor was Herbert ever friendly with him again, even refusing to see him when he called at his home for some business reason.

The quartet lasted altogether three years. Its programs were selected from classical chamber music, with a leaning toward the lighter compositions and transcriptions.

Herbert always played his parts like a virtuoso, but with one number he had difficulty. That was the Beethoven A minor Quartet, in which the cello part in the last movement goes so high as to be in the violin register. They played it at a concert in the Carnegie Chamber Music Hall, and in the intermission before the last movement, the other players saw Herbert take three swigs from a bottle of whisky he carried in his pocket.

VI

So active was Herbert in propagating his talents, that only seven years after he arrived in New York he was called to lead the Twenty-second Regiment Band of New York, better known to musical history as Gilmore's Band. After the death of the famous bandmaster, Patrick Saarsfield Gilmore, his band was under the direction of Walter Reeves for two years. But the men were dissatisfied and sought a new conductor. The name of Victor Herbert was suggested at a meeting and at once approved. A committee was dispatched to confer with him, and he accepted the post.

This action was the beginning of his break with serious music. To lead even as noted a band as Gilmore's was a step down for a man who had been assistant conductor to Anton Seidl, and who had established himself as a virtuoso concert cellist.

Gilmore's was a regimental band, and of course it had to play at parades and all military functions. Its concerts appealed exclusively to the popular tastes, as all bands necessarily do.

But this band was famous and Herbert wanted fame. The designation, "Leader of Gilmore's Band," attracted him. The glitter of the uniform, too, was to his taste. Then Gilmore's Band had a concert following and also did a large business playing at dances, especially those given by society leaders. It was a good proposition.

The only difficulty Herbert found in transferring himself to band music was that he demanded of the clarinets the same agility possessed by violins. This brought an occasional *impasse* between him and his men, if he arranged the music. But he quickly mastered the new technique, and conducting a military band became one of his accomplishments.

It was Gilmore's Band, with Victor Herbert conducting, that played the dances at the Bradley-Martin costume ball, in the old Waldorf-Astoria Hotel, probably the most sensational social event ever held in this country. It cost a fortune, and its purpose was to outdo all the other balls ever given by New York society queens.

The grandiose affair took place February 10, 1897. It was during a period of depression, and when it became known that Mrs. Bradley-Martin planned to exhaust all the flower shops of the state to festoon the ballroom, and that the costumes to be worn by the guests would run into enough money to feed a town for a week, indignant cries began to be heard all over the city and then throughout the country. Rather surprised at this reception of their idea the Bradley-Martins let it be known that the ball was being held with the object of stimulating trade and that the money spent on it would go into circulation for the benefit of others. This struck some people as funny, and others as stupidly arrogant. The city began to seethe with discussion of the projected festivity.

Mrs. Bradley-Martin, however, went ahead with her plans, and because Gilmore's Band was the foremost organization of its kind, it was engaged.

Herbert had to bring his men over to the Astor mansion for rehearsal of the elaborate dances, and Seidl's assistant conductor carefully went over measure after measure as the most distinguished members of the Four Hundred got their toes in proper step and their bodies into the required swing.

The ball was held amid the greatest excitement. There was a mob outside the Waldorf which required a cordon of police to hold in order. From the *Times* is the following breathless description of the affair over which Herbert presided with his music:

"The grand ballroom was a scene of splendor. The eye scarcely knew where to look or what to study, it was such a bewildering maze of gorgeous dames and gentlemen on the floor, in such a flood of light from the ceiling, paneled in terra-cotta and gold, and such an entrancing picture of garlands that hung everywhere in rich festoons.

"The first impression on entering the room was that some fairy godmother, in a dream, had revived the glories of the past for one's special enjoyment, and that one was mingling with the dignitaries of ancient régimes, so perfect was the illusion.

"Then the strains of the dance began. Where did they come from? On the south end of the ballroom one saw nothing but a wild riot of flowers and vines. They covered the balcony, which is divided into five sections. But the only way to tell this was by counting the superb displays of garlands that hung from one section to another, interlaced and backed with a solid bank of galax, that rich, dark leaf gathered in South Carolina from the hillsides. Over this was a lacework of the long-stemmed pink roses, interwined with the most lavish abandon, and forming a floral screen in front of the balcony. Behind this were the musicians, a string band of fifty pieces (this was the traditional 'Hungarian' orchestra that played the incidental music; Herbert's band was used for the dances). The opposite side of the room was one of special splendor. Imbedded in the wall are sixteen large mirrors. They were not hidden from view—that would never do— but from the walls above them were hanging gorgeous interlaced festoons of orchids and asparagus vines. They were mauve orchids, those floral aristocrats of the orchid family, chosen to grace this occasion, because of their acknowledged standing in the world of flowers.

"Curious ornaments hung from the sixteen candelabra on the north side of the room. They were made in imitation of the pouches or huge reticules the ladies used to wear in the days of Louis XVI—large pocket-like concerns of blue silk and alternately filled with pink roses and orchids. As the guests sauntered along that side of the room, or sat and chatted in the dainty chairs of white and gold, these garlands of orchids and asparagus and these pockets with the floral treasures hung over them like a canopy and gave a superb festival effect to the glittering scene."

It was conservatively estimated that five thousand roses and three thousand orchids were used in the decorations of the ballroom. Three thousand orchids! They must have made Herbert's republican Irish heart miss some beats.

An ironic sequel to the ball was that this great display of wealth caused the city to raise Mr. Bradley-Martin's taxes, whereupon he became so enraged that he went abroad to live.

One of Herbert's men who played with him at the ball—Otto Schreiber—relates that between the dances Herbert was introduced to many of the guests. But another of the old bandsmen who was there has no recollection that Herbert was so privileged. He does remember, however, that while the bandsmen ate in the officers' hall, Herbert was not with them. That was unusual. At affairs like that Herbert preferred to eat at one table with his men.

Herbert always had the affection of his bandsmen because they thought him "so democratic." To them he was a great genius, a man who had come to a band from the heights of grand opera and symphony societies graced by Seidl and Thomas.

Because of his bulk, Herbert perspired profusely and the less clothes he had on the better he liked it. His men, therefore, as often saw him in his underwear as in his uniform, and this, alone, added to his renown for being "one of the boys."

His anxiety to be comfortable by shedding as much clothing as he could while working is the basis of a good story. Fritz Stahlberg, who later was one of Herbert's conductors, visited him one day in his private quarters at the resort where his band was playing. It was a hot summer day and Herbert was sitting at a table writing music. He was clad only in his B.V.D.'s and that garment was wide open all the way down the front. Stahlberg remarked that that was a good way to work.

"Yes, it is," Herbert agreed. "But there's one drawback to it."

"What?" Stahlberg asked.

"The God-damned hot ashes from my cigar keep dropping down where they shouldn't."

Every February the first, Herbert's birthday, his men gathered in front of his home and serenaded him. The entire street was aroused by this mammoth German street band blowing away on the sidewalk and stamping their feet in the snow. Herbert would respond with a beaming face, and then bring the entire crowd into his home, where kegs of beer were enthroned in the dining-room and Mrs. Herbert had prepared great platters of cold meats. Not many set speeches were made. Such occasions were for eating and drinking.

"We had no time for speeches," Somerset, the bandsman, recalls. "Not while the kegs and the plates held out."

Another celebration was always held on St. Patrick's Day. But this came later, when Herbert had his orchestra. On that famous day all the players would turn up with green ties.

In both his bands and orchestras, Herbert had a special factotum whose chief business, when the band was touring, was to carry a big wicker lunch basket. It was filled with all sorts of cold cuts, cheeses and Herbert's idolized imported Pilsener beer. The basket was never allowed to get empty. It was the reserve in case Herbert did not have time to eat at a restaurant, or anything else interfered with his regular meals.

The leading basket-bearer was a Bavarian tuba player called Thome. He was of the true servant class and enjoyed his commission and carefully preserved it. He had as regular an allowance from Herbert to keep the basket properly replenished as a cook in a household has from her mistress for kitchen needs.

One of Herbert's great pleasures in connection with the band was to lead it at parades. He took a naïve pride in marching at the head of his men, his large head held high and his face beaming on the crowd lining the curbs. He even frequently took the hallowed place of the drum major, sending that disappointed individual back to the drum corps. Sometimes he made his little son, Clifford, join him in these ceremonials, dressed in a miniature uniform.

The importance of Gilmore's Band at that time is further indicated by its engagement for the official ball in Washington which followed President McKinley's inauguration, March 4, 1897. The ball did not cost as much as the Bradley-Martin affair—only fifty thousand dollars—but it was resplendent with diplomatic color, and Herbert was in his glory as, in a new uniform, he led his men in the music for the dances. Two days later he took advantage of the distinction he had received by giving a concert in Carnegie Hall, mentioning emphatically in the advertising that he and his men had just returned from the inauguration ceremonies.

Herbert arranged and wrote much music for the band, and his men marveled at his facility. There is one particular example of his virtuosity in this direction. While playing in Washington Park, New Jersey, one of the cornet players was struck by the idea of having three cornetists play the "Lizzie Polka" as a trio. Hagar, Clark and Schmidt (not Louis) were the cornetists and they came to Herbert with the plan.

"But it isn't arranged for three cornets," he objected.

"We'll play it in unison," they replied.

"No, that won't do," said Herbert. "I don't think the 'Lizzie Polka' is good for the purpose, either. I'll write you a new piece."

That was before the afternoon concert. After the performance Herbert went to his room and that evening he had ready a three-part piece called "The Three Solitaires." It was played by the men at the night concert and became a standard number with Gilmore's Band.

Herbert rarely had any trouble with his men, but on one occasion such serious friction developed that he was suspended by the Musicians' Union.

This incident occurred near the end of his leadership

of the band. Gilmore's was run as a business organization and Herbert's interest in it was his retainer and
a share of the profits. The regiment to which it was
attached merely paid for its use at military functions.

Herbert took the band for a tour of the South and
the returns were insufficient to pay the men in full.
Although they were fond of their leader, a number of
them forgot some of their affection and considered that
Herbert was obligated to pay them from his own
pocket. Herbert denied that, claiming that he had
nothing to do with the expenses of the organization.

The matter was taken up with the Union. They
found Herbert guilty and suspended him without notice. The case caused a factional fight among musicians,
but Herbert took no action, thinking he was above the
squabble. However, soon after this, he was asked by
the Lambs Club, of which he was an ardent member,
to lead a concert for them, and when he tried to engage
his men for the event the Union refused permission.
He offered to pay whatever fines were imposed on the
musicians for playing with him, but the men were
afraid of the risk and so Herbert had to suffer the hu-
miliation of seeing some one else conduct the Lambs'
concert.

The threat of a legal battle caused the Union to
reconsider its action, and soon it was announced that
Herbert had paid the claim charged against him and
was reinstated to full membership. This, however,
was not entirely true, for Herbert had not paid the
claim.

On March 28, 1898, Anton Seidl died. He was only forty-eight and his death was a great shock to all his friends, to whom it seemed unbelievable that such a dynamic person could pass away so simply. His death came suddenly. A doctor diagnosed his illness as ptomaine poisoning caused by the eating of shad roe which, "in some exceptionally rare cases," as the physician put it, "develops in the springtime a deadly poison, so much more deadly since it cannot be detected by sight, taste or smell."

The funeral was held on March 31, and a memorial service was conducted in the Metropolitan. On its way to the opera house the cortège was met, at Fortieth Street and Fifth Avenue, by a hundred members of the Musicians' Union, under the direction of Victor Herbert and Nahan Franko. They acted as a funeral band and preceded the hearse, playing the poignant Beethoven funeral march. It was the one parade through the streets of New York in which Herbert took part with a sad face.

Later he wrote a tribute to his famous friend which embodies some interesting personal recollections. It follows:

"When I came to the United States, in 1886, I had known Anton Seidl by his great reputation as a Wagner disciple, then so widespread in Europe. He was at that time in the second year of his work at the Metropolitan Opera House. The musicians comprising his orchestra had readily come to appreciate his profound knowledge of Beyreuth tradition, alike of the stage and the orchestra. They found in Seidl a man thoroughly imbued with Wagner's ideas, both in general conception and in the smallest detail of each opera. He fairly bristled with animated energy and was ever on the alert to right the minutest of errors. His thorough knowledge of this work, which with him was a life passion, enabled Seidl to make incredible progress with both players and singers in preparation of his superb productions. The great presentation of 'Tristan and Isolde' at the Metropolitan Opera House in the year of my arrival was accomplished with but five rehearsals with the orchestra, including the one set apart for the correction of the orchestral parts.

"But our conductor never took to himself any credit for such remarkable achievements. Always anxious to ascribe honor where honor was due, he attributed this, the greatest success of the season, to perfection of discipline in the orchestra, the ready perception of its members and their fine routine in orchestral work. To his soloists he was ever anxious to accord a full measure of praise. In 1886, for instance, the principals included Lehman, Auguste Kraus (Seidl's wife), Marianne Brandt, Niemann, Robinson, Anton Schott, Alvary and Herbert-Foerster, whose artistic contributions to these great operatic performances were graciously recognized by the conductor, his characteristic modesty invariably placing them and the orchestra before himself.

"The musicians frequently saw that the music affected Seidl most profoundly. He was a man of deep emotion. Certain passages in 'Seigfried,' and the wonderful closing scene of 'Tristan,' always made him cry like a child, so that by the time the curtain dropped he would be in a state of emotional collapse.

"Seidl was universally admired and loved by the members of his orchestra. He never showed the faintest trace of false pride. His players were his companions, his helpers; he was simply one of them. It was through this strong bond of fraternity that he came to acquire a powerful personal influence over the instrumentalists which was entirely distinct from the musical magnetism exerted in rehearsals and public performances. This all-powerful, impelling yet unfathomable power of control imperiously commanded his followers in the orchestra by first awakening their entire interest and then spurring them on to efforts that they could make under the baton of no other master. The graceful, incisive, clean-cut movements of his stick were intelligible at all times. And, for his part, Seidl always relied implicitly upon the quick perception of his musicians, never wasting time in unnecessary explanations of what was to be brought about in this bar, or avoided in that. We always knew by a glance from his eye what was expected of us.

"Mr. Seidl was a man little given to words. As it was so aptly remarked of Von Moltke's position in the realm of scientific warfare, so may it be said of Anton Seidl as a musician and conductor, that he was 'der grosse Schweiger' (the great Silent). Yet he never failed to say the right thing in the right place and many anecdotes are related of his quick wit and dry humor. When he talked it was because he had something to say; and, as many of his friends can attest, he was exceptionally apt in his remarks.

"Some years since, after a performance of his orchestra at Brighton Beach, a few of us sat down towards midnight for a lunch with Mr. Seidl in his favorite café. There were present in the little party several musicians, and among the enthusiastic amateurs of music, a prominent New York manufacturer who was an ardent admirer of Italian opera. For twoscore years or more this gentleman faithfully attended all the Italian opera presentations in New York; he had fraternized with all the famous artists who sallied from their Milan stronghold to make conquests of the New World audiences. As one would naturally expect, during the course of the evening he turned the drift of conversation upon the subject of his favorite hobby. Niemann was present, and, if I mistake not, there may have been another singer or two in the little gathering.

"All save Seidl had something to say about the decadence of the ultramontane school of opera. Finally, when the subject seemed to have been exhausted, the conductor made a few remarks.

"He was known to be very fair in his judgment of men and their works. He admired all that was good in Italian operatic music, but was ready to condemn what was rubbish. Many of the singers from sunny Italy he regarded as great; Campanini's glorious voice and superb vocal art were his especial admiration. But his profound regard for the eternal fitness of things appeared to instigate this brief, succinct expression of his views on the topic under discussion:

" 'In the property room of the Metropolitan House, gentlemen, there is a helmet.' He paused for a moment, reflectively puffed at his cigar, and then resumed: 'It may be tarnished now, but a year or two ago it was brightly burnished. If you were to hunt it up you would find that this specimen is much like other helmets save for the "Schwanritter" emblem which it bears. It was made for "Lohengrin," and my dear friend Campanini wore it in a truly magnificent performance of the rôle. Yet if you were to find that helmet to-day you would discover that in addition to the prescribed dimensions and insignia of this piece of knightly headgear, Mr. Campanini had put on a blue plume, probably three feet in length. That, my dear gentlemen, is Italian opera.'

"Seidl's death was the pathetic termination of a career which had just fairly realized its highest ambitions. He had just come into the acquisition of all that he had hoped for. Strong influence had secured for Seidl a substantially permanent orchestra. This was a well-deserved recognition of his merits and talents. He had the Philharmonic Society and the Metropolitan Opera House German productions. He had the promise of regular work at Beyreuth festivals; and a permanent engagement at Covent Garden, in London. And in the midst of all this, the ripe harvest of a busy life, Seidl was stricken down."

It is easy to see Seidl's influence in Victor Herbert's life.

Herbert was known as a strict disciplinarian at rehearsals or concerts, even though he was ready to fraternize with his men at all other times. He could catch the slightest error in performance and knew just what he wanted. He had a great knowledge of the orchestra and this saved him much time in preparation. In all these things he was akin to Seidl, and the probability is that he carefully studied his master and patterned himself after him.

Herbert was courtly and considerate in introducing his wife's name into this tribute. No doubt he was proud that his wife had once been one of Seidl's singers. But always he could be relied upon to do the courtly thing in public where a woman was concerned.

He was driving one afternoon in a carriage with his friend, Henry Burck, and a friend of Burck's, Mrs. Taber. The lady was handling the horses and they were going along at a smart pace when she fumbled to take out her handkerchief. Herbert produced his own fresh handkerchief and gave it to her. Later Mrs. Taber returned the piece of linen, laundered, and Herbert sent it back, as a souvenir, with a few measures of his song, "Kiss Me," gallantly written on it.

VII

AFTER his wife left the Metropolitan Opera House, Herbert was often in strained circumstances. Joseph Weber, of the Musicians' Union, relates that one afternoon he and the composer were walking along Fourth Avenue in the Madison Square neighborhood and Herbert pointed out a building to him.

"There was once a time," the composer said, "when I could not pay the eighteen dollars a week rent in that place."

But he found his social level almost at once, and thereafter kept himself within that genial and clever circle of professional intellectuals known to outsiders as Bohemians.

James Huneker mentions him several times in his autobiographical book, "Steeplejack." Of the period of about 1886 (the first year the Herberts were in America), he says:

"I breathed an atmosphere ozone-charged. The idols of my youth were to be seen perambulating Irving Place, Union Square, Fourteenth Street. At Lienau's you might see William Steinway in the flesh, an immense political influence, as well as a musical. Theodore Thomas lived on East Seventeenth Street, opposite the Garrigues. William Mason would alight from the little blue horse-car which ran across Seventeenth

Street, at Union Square. He lived in Orange, New Jersey, and always stopped at Brubacher's, where he met S. B. Mills, before beginning his lessons at Steinway Hall. A polished pianist, a delightful raconteur, Mr. Mason could discourse by the hour about Franz Liszt, with whom he had studied. And then there were to be seen at Lienau's, Anton Seidl, Mr. and Mrs. Charles F. Tretbar, Nahum Stetson, Jossefy, Sternberg, Rummel, Scharwenka, Lilli Lehman, Van der Stucken, Krehbiel, Mr. and Mrs. Victor Herbert, Rosenthal, Mr. and Mrs. Ferdinand von Inten, Charles S. Steinway and of course Max Hinrich. A few doors down the block was Augustus Lüchow's restaurant, which outlived Lienau's and a host of other hostelries."

He then relates that he got lodgings in the neighborhood.

"A small family hotel at the northeast corner of Irving Place and Seventeenth Street, kept by an elderly couple, was noted for its cooking and cheerfulness. Werle's, too, was an artistic rendezvous and its table-d'hôte dinners saw many celebrities. There were always entertaining companions. It was one of those houses where at any time before midnight the sound of pianos, violins, violincellos, even the elegaic flute, might be heard, and usually played by skilled musicians. There was also much vocal squawking. Across the street was, and still is, the pretty Washington Irving house and at another corner lived Victor Herbert. From the vine-covered entrance of Werle's I often heard string music made by Victor Herbert, Max Bendix—then concert-master of the Thomas Orchestra, and a Philadelphian—and others. I occupied on the ground floor a room about as big as the one I lived in in Paris. It held a bed, an upright piano, a trunk, some books and music. It had one advantage, it was easy of access, and one disadvantage—I never knew when I would be alone. Friends knocked on the window with their sticks at all hours of the night. They also sang concerted noises. Finally I stayed out on purpose till dawn to escape their intrusions."

And in penning a nostalgic note on the old Steinway Hall (now so fantastically replaced with a cut-rate dress shop and blaring radio and novelty emporiums), Huneker recalled:

"Steinway Hall was once the resort of our crowd, composed of Harry Rowe Shelley, Harry Orville Brown, Henry Junge, John Kiehl, Jossefy, Friedheim, Max Bendix, Victor Herbert and, when in town, the witty Moriz Rosenthal."

Huneker and Herbert were good friends, though later in their careers they did not see much of each other. Huneker was always an idealist and could not deviate from the path he had chosen; Herbert was not so steadfast.

Mrs. Huneker declares that her husband lost much of his interest in Herbert when the latter told him, at about the time he began to make the transition from serious music to comic opera:

"You can keep to your ideals, Jim. I want to make money."

Herbert once expressed the same decision in another form to Walter Damrosch. Speaking about his music, he said:

"I am going to write comic operas until I make enough to write what I want."

Huneker piloted the young Irish-American cellist to many of the Bohemian haunts and they frequented the same places for about fifteen years. An appetizing picture of those beer and food paradises which formed much of Herbert's social background, is contained in a volume of autobiography which deserves to be better known than it is, at least for its chapters on old New York life. It is "A Solitary Parade," written by Frederick L. Hackenburg, a lawyer of the metropolis and a friend of Huneker's.

"Down at Hanover Square," Hackenburg writes, "across from India House, a vicinity rich with historical associations of early New York merchants, among towering office buildings and ramshackle old warehouses scented with the odor of Old-World drugs and Oriental spices, there existed in the days before the War, a large beer saloon. A queer place, roomy, dark, comfortable, frequented by the cosmopolitan crowd from the neighboring shipping offices, it had a distinctly German atmosphere.

"During the evening hours Knirim's Pilsener Sanatorium was a favorite hangout for all the ship reporters from their nearby headquarters at Battery Park.

"Old man Knirim, sparse, large, with a Teutonic cast of countenance and a strong German accent, moved

with silent step among his crowd of witty guests, a ther-
mometer in hand, testing the temperature of each individual glass of Pilsener. Knirim was a philosopher,
versed in the abstract thinking of the metaphysical
school of reasoning; his favorite theory was that hu-
manity was going to the damnation bow-wows by drinking cold beer. The temperature of his Pilsener had to
be kept at lukewarm point. Drinking cold beer was a
sin against culture, an offense against reason, an act of
stupid ignorance, a display of barbarism. The boys
used to have a lot of fun getting him started on this
favorite topic.

"In his younger days Knirim had kept a saloon somewhere near the entrance to Brooklyn Bridge. It had
been the headquarters of the German revolutionaries.
Herr Johann Most had frequented the place. When
Knirim died he made a bequest to Lenin's widow to
assure all posterity that he was protesting against the
existing order of things even by a final gesture from
beyond his grave.

"A regular habitué of the Hanover Square place was
James Huneker, the critic and iconoclast. I picked up
his acquaintance there. Old Knirim, a rabid dissenter
from all adopted standards, with the true spirit of an-
archy burning in his Pilsener-loving soul, had only
contempt for anybody's literary (or any other kind, for
that matter) views. However, he and Huneker became
fast friends by reason of their common, ardent, nearly
religious adoration of the amber-colored fluid that made
Pilsen famous.

"To watch the two of them standing at the end of the enormous bar, slowly imbibing the life-giving nectar, the enjoyment of a true devotee oozing from every pore of their bodies, was the most inspiring argument against prohibition that I can remember.

"At this particular period I formed a habit of dropping in at the saloon on frequent evenings, attracted both by the quality of the beverage and by the interesting talk of the frequenters. After the place had closed for the night I walked on many occasions up to Fourteenth Street with Huneker, continuing our conversations about things in general and nothing in particular, discussing Nietzsche, Schopenhauer, Max Nordau, Stirner and his ego, or listening to Huneker's prose poems about his main hobby and purpose in life, Chopin's music.

"We would turn into Lüchow's and refresh our parched throats with another glass or two of genuine Pilsener (cold, this time, notwithstanding all the preachments of Knirim); and we would leave Fourteenth Street and start on the next lap of our pilgrimage towards our homes in Yorkville, making another stop on the way in East Fifty-eighth Street, at Terrace Garden, where the conversation was charming and the Pilsener acceptable to the connoisseur's palate.

"They still make real Pilsener in Pilsen, but Knirim's and Lüchow's and the Terrace Garden are just shadows of memory. Old Knirim is gone. Old Lüchow, too, although they still run the restaurant and sell near-beer there in profanation of the past. Old Adolph

Sueskind, the genial host at Terrace Garden, also has joined the big procession. Huneker, the easy-going, with a poet's soul and a brewer's shape, left this vale of tears soon after the War brought to a stop the importation of Pilsener brew across the blockaded deep. One stormy night in the early part of April, 1915, while a wild gale was blowing around the street corners, splashing sheets of rain-water into the very laps of adventurous pedestrians brave enough to face the storm, I walked into the deserted place down at Hanover Street. The sole waiter on duty was dozing in a chair behind the bar. I heard a murmur of voices from the region of the cellar. I walked down the stairs. Under the flickering light of a single candle, fastened in the neck of an old bottle which stood on a broken box, a scene that I will never forget presented itself to my astonished eyes.

"Sad and dejected stood the two towering figures of Huneker and Knirim. In an attitude of pall-bearers at the funeral of a departed friend they were tapping the last keg of Pilsener in Knirim's cellar. Imbued with the solemnity of the grave moment, fully aware of the ghastly fate descending upon us in a cruel world empty of all Pilsener, I joined the mourners."

The Terrace Garden was one of Herbert's prized halting places. In summer, an orchestra, conducted by his friend, Paul Hennenberg, played there. After the success of his first operettas, with his pockets filled with money, it was a joyous recreation with Herbert to drop in at the Terrace Garden, take out a wad of bills, slap them under his right elbow and exclaim: "All right, boys!" This was the signal for a general treat while the orchestra played his favorite pieces.

But of all the places popular with New York Bohemians, Herbert was more often in Lüchow's. Mindful of the history of this place one looks upon it tearfully to-day. It still is located in the same place, Fourteenth Street, near Fourth Avenue. It still has the same old-world appearance it had then. But what a change in the surroundings! A bazaar of cheap, loud stores, a burlesque theater, movie houses, an incongruous skyscraper, an automat restaurant, groups of embittered Communists, nondescript crowds. Gone is Steinway Hall, gone the Academy of Music, gone the community of writers, musicians and artists that clustered around that portion of O. Henry's Bagdad-on-the-Subway.

They still remember Victor Herbert at Lüchow's. Old Gus Lüchow is now in Valhalla, but a relative of his, Victor Eckstein, who manages the restaurant, will sing a rhapsody of the dishes Herbert liked best.

Eckstein remembers when Lüchow's delivered regular shipments of imported beer to Herbert's home and when the composer used to arrive, surrounded by a crowd of friends and mere acquaintances he had picked up on the way down. He recalls the famous musician's beatific look of pleasure as a valued dish was lowered slowly from the waiter's respectful hands and passed before his sensitive nose.

Herbert was a connoisseur of foods—mostly German

foods—and while he was a large eater, he was an appreciative one. Eckstein itemizes an almost complete list of the epicure's favorite dishes:

"Boiled beef with horse-radish sauce and wine kraut. Wine kraut is sauerkraut steamed with Rhine wine. Very marvelous."

(Picture an Irishman eating beef and wined sauerkraut!)

"Veal chops *au naturel*. This is a plain veal chop—that is, it is cooked without any ingredient to take away from its flavor. It is just fried in butter and not a bread crumb touches it.

"Ragout of tenderloin beef and fresh mushrooms.

"*Weiner Rostbratten*. This is a sirloin steak fried over charcoal with grated horse-radish, onions and potatoes spread over it. The potatoes, please remember, are fried raw, not cooked first.

"Hamburger *Kucken*. A squab chicken which is potted in butter and baked over a slow fire.

"Hamburger steak. The kind Herbert liked was prepared differently from the ordinary Hamburger, composed of chopped fresh beef, onions and marrow and fried in butter. Herbert liked it medium rare.

"He was fond of planked veal steak, which is the meat broiled on a plank, surrounded with cauliflower, peas, beans, asparagus and mushrooms.

"He liked very much onion soup and *kraftsuppe*. *Kraftsuppe* is a soup made of double strength consommé, potatoes, marrow (which is taken out of the bone and cooked with the soup), and a slice of boiled beef and parsley. The onion soup is double strength consommé cooked with onions in individual stone pots. When the soup is ready it is put in the oven and baked and then served in the individual pots.

"He liked meat more than fish, but he enjoyed these fish dishes: Boiled haddock and mustard butter, which is a sauce made of drawn butter and mustard (the butter is melted in a double boiler and whipped); boiled pompano with potatoes boiled, dipped in butter and rolled in parsley; English sole (imported from the North Sea), fried in butter; boiled fresh sturgeon steak and potato salad.

"He did not care much for sweets or fruits but he liked apple pancakes and pancakes with imported cranberries. In both these dishes the fruit is spread on a baked crust made of flour, water and eggs, the finished crust being first covered with cinnamon and sugar.

"Of liquors he drank Pilsener and Wurtzburger beer, and if he had wine it was generally Moselle."

From Henry Burck, one of his orchestra players and intimates, is gathered some additional items of the Herbert menu. Burck says that when Herbert came to New York he lived first in a boarding house north of Times Square. It was kept by a German lady, and patronized mostly by German professionals. There Herbert luxuriated in the kind of food for which he developed such a great taste during the years he lived in Germany.

For desserts, according to Burck, Herbert was fond of *mehlspeise,* a term for warm strudels and puddings.

One of such dishes consists of noodles mixed with poppyseed and sugar. Herbert was particularly fond of kraut strudel, a delicate dessert made of cabbage rolled in pastry dough.

In addition to Moselle, Herbert liked a German wine called "Berncastler Doktor." At the memory of it, Burck rolls his eyes and sighs: "It was heaven!"

When he was thirsty, Herbert drank claret and water. Plain water seemed to him a vulgar way of quenching thirst.

He preserved his liking for food all his life and always finished his plate. Until he reached his later years he tempered his eating and drinking with exercise. He was a good walker and could make five or six miles without exertion. In the mornings he religiously attended to calesthenics, and so strong was his constitution that even after staying up late working, or being otherwise occupied, he would rise fresh in the morning and feeling so grand his voice could be heard carolling throughout the house, interspersed with exuberant chords and runs on the piano.

But for about the last five years of his life he discarded exercise. His doctor, Emanuel Baruch, declares that this neglect probably hastened his end.

Good food and good drinks were essential to Herbert's nature and were in natural harmony with his good-fellowship. He was gayest at the dinner table and at the banquets given in his honor, or in honor of others. Always he was the life of the party.

He belonged to an exclusive little musical organization called the Rubato Club. Herbert's entertainments there are still fondly remembered by survivors. His admission to the closed circle was made a festive occasion at which he was presented with a loving cup in the form of a chamber pot. From this he drank the celebration liquor, and the other members followed him in turn. Then a specially composed song was sung, of which the following are a few of the many verses:

> "To-night we initiate the first
>   New member in the Club.
> O Victor Herbert, you're a brick,
>   You're welcomed by this mob.
>
> Here all of us we know quite well,
>   That Victor likes to treat;
> He'll do it morning, noon and night,
>   He'd rather treat than eat.
>
> To-day he writes an opera,
>   To-morrow a symphonie;
> He plays the violincello and
>   He leads the Philharmonie.
>
> To Herbert's versatility
>   There is no end, by Joe;
> He's General Utility,
>   He's always on the go."

At one of the Rubato festivals, Fritz Kreisler sang a song about a Viennese dandy and Herbert responded with one of his most famous private contributions, a song about the hallowed loves of a stable boy and a farm girl. The boy was an honest soul with a romantic heart. Nature inspired him, and whenever he heard the cow moo or the pig grunt he was moved to think of his love.

Herbert had a fair baritone, and when his voice reached down to the bass of the pig's grunt or to the contralto of the cow's moo his listeners heard a first-rate vaudeville comic.

A German dialect story he told was also celebrated. He was fond of the Swabians and had mastered their talk perfectly. The Swabians are a very courteous people, and Herbert related that a group of passengers were in the waiting room of a railroad station in Swabia when the station-master came in and politely called out:

"Is there any one here left for Oberbamflingeh?"

After a pause he informed:

"I ask this because I should like to inform you the train has just left."

Much of the humor in this tale lay in Herbert's perfection as a Swabian dialectician. He, of course, spoke German as fluently as English. He also had a knowledge of other languages, being able to switch from one tongue to another when rehearsing his internationally blended orchestras.

He spoke German exclusively with his wife, and he dropped into that language when he was with people who knew it. This had some effect on his English, a slight accent being noticeable. But whether his accent was German or Irish his listeners found it hard to determine, so vague was it. The compromise decision is that when he was angry the accent became definitely one or the other.

It was also in the days that prefaced the real Victor
Herbert that he met the Irishmen who brought him
once more close to his national heritage. As a grandson of Samuel Lover, he attracted the attention of his
compatriots. He met and became friends with the old
Fenians of the city, men like O'Donovan Rossa and
John Devoy, the city editor of the *New York Herald*,
author of a poem, "The Fighting Race," which he was
called upon to recite at all Irish gatherings. Herbert
also became a lifelong friend of Judge Daniel Cohalan.

All these men turned his Irish patriotism, which had
been dormant during his German period, into a mili-
tant direction. England and the English became fixed
aversions with him. His Irish feelings, however, were
derived from the emotions rather than from thoughtful
consideration. He would find more truth in a phrase
like, "those God-damned bastards!" than in an analytical study of English-Irish relations.

Curiously enough, despite his intimate Irish associations in New York, he could never develop a fancy
for Irish food. The Irish national dish of bacon or
corned beef and cabbage had absolutely no allure for
Victor Herbert.

VIII

AFTER he had been conducting Gilmore's Band for some time, and as he was more drawn into providing popular music, Herbert's thoughts turned strongly to the stage.

In his boyhood and young manhood, Offenbach's operettas had been popular, and the success of that French composer—also a cellist, by the way—was one of the "inspirational" stories of the day. Later came Gilbert and Sullivan, their operas earning fortunes for their creators.

Herbert felt pressed by two forces: there was the strong desire to make enough money to realize his ideas of good living; there was the almost subconscious craving to express his lightness of spirit in melody, a craving which went hand in hand with an affinity for the glamour of the theatre.

With serious music one didn't make much money in those days. The most popular singers or violinists or pianists could obtain handsome rewards for their artistry, but neither cellists nor conductors had much financial scope. Even the great Seidl was in difficulties much of the time.

Herbert was well aware of this, and his aggressive nature made him impatient of his position. He was in his mid-thirties. His reputation was mainly as a cello

Victor Herbert as Leader of Gilmore's Band.

Victor Herbert, in His Cello Virtuoso Days, with a Group
of Friends. Louis Schmidt is at the Extreme Right.

soloist and conductor. He had written considerable music in all forms—nearly all of it published in Germany—but while his works were favorably received, they were considered of no greater importance than the early efforts of a prolific composer of energy and promise.

The work of Herbert's that attracted most attention in this period was a cantata written for the Worcester, Mass., festival of 1891. It is now a forgotten work, for in it Herbert's melodiousness was subordinated to the seriousness of a purpose. The result was a heavy, massively scored composition of superficial emotions, with only short sections of worth-while music—as the first part of the closing chorus.

It was, however, an American work. Patriotic pride, stirred by a piece containing professional finesse, inspired good notices. H. E. Krehbiel, later to develop into a noted critic, gave it high praise. He wrote in a *New York Tribune* review, September 25, 1891:

"Mr. Herbert, who sprouted in Dublin, budded in Stuttgart and blossomed in New York, was to-day classed with the American composers. He could not be better recommended to the guild than he was by his cantata, 'The Captive.' The work was sadly mutilated in the performance, it being found necessary to omit one of its strongest divisions, because of the inability of the choir to learn the music in time; but despite these drawbacks a composition full of dramatic virility and beauty was recognizable. The textual framework of 'The Captive' is a German poem by

Rudolph Baumbach, which tells the tale of a prisoner condemned to death, whom a maiden wishes to save for her love, but who prefers death to infidelity to his mistress. Mr. Herbert's setting of the lines is ultra-modern in form and style. The poem is largely narrative and in these portions Mr. Herbert has adopted a dramatically tinctured choral-ballad manner, leaving this, however, for something like highly emotionalized, or even higher spiced, operatic expression, in the portions in which direct characterization is possible. That is to say he sets the words supposed to be spoken by the captive and the love-stricken maiden as solos.

"The narrative and individual elements, as well as the conflicting passions of the hero and heroine, have typical themes in the score, and these themes are the melodic gems of the work. In the instrumental introduction they are stated so as to suggest the argument of the story and at the same time furnish a sort of thematic catalogue. The freedom of Mr. Herbert's fancy does a kind of work which would seem to belong to the domain of reflection in this elaboration; and in spite of the incapacity of the choir, he was made to feel that his composition had received both professional and popular appreciation."

Herbert acted in several capacities at this festival as this paragraph from another of Krehbiel's criticisms shows:

"The instrumental numbers in the afternoon's scheme (on the second day of the festival), besides the symphony of Schumann, were the andante and pizzicato scherzo from Tschaikovsky's Symphony in F minor, Grieg's 'Peer Gynt' music and Saint-Saën's Concerto in A minor for violincello. This concerto was played by Victor Herbert, who is factotum in ordinary to the festival: assistant conductor, pianoforte accompanist and commissioned composer. In the last capacity he will appear to-morrow afternoon, when an ambitious work for solo voices, chorus and orchestra entitled 'The Captive' will have its first performance. As a virtuoso on his chosen instrument he gave great pleasure to-day, though I fear that all the concerto, except a daintily conceived middle part, was caviar to the general."

The conductor whom Herbert assisted was Carl Zerrahn.

It should be noted that "The Captive" was performed at the same concert at which, for the first time, was heard McDowell's orchestral suite in A minor. No doubt Herbert had a hand in its preparation. McDowell had been invited to attend but refused, being unwilling, Krehbiel thought, to be classed as an "American composer," a personality which this concert aimed to exploit.

Krehbiel grew enthusiastic over another composition of Herbert's, a "Serenade for Strings," performed December 1, 1888, at one of Seidl's concerts. He wrote:

"Mr. Herbert's composition was written for strings and the performance was conducted by him. It won for him the heartiest applause of the evening. Less interesting for its melodies (some of which have familiar faces) than for the manner in which they were handled, the 'Serenade' is nevertheless a composition which deserves to be played again. The vivid and varied slashes of color which Mr. Herbert threw into the score, notwithstanding that he had only five stringed instruments of the orchestra at his command, were most effective. One movement, the third, I should like to see taken out of the set by Mr. Herbert and rewritten for full band. It is denominated 'A Love Scene,' and in it Mr. Herbert develops an intensity of feeling which, though eloquently expressed by the voices of the quintet, deserves a larger and more telling apparatus."

This praise was more warranted, for Herbert was always happiest when writing for the orchestra, or any division of it. His skill for achieving arresting and charming instrumental effects was widely known.

Some of his works appeared here and there at this time: a "Berceuse and Polonaise," for cello, played by himself at a private concert in 1887; a song at a Mendelssohn Glee Club concert, "Ah, Love Me!" sung by Mrs. Marie Gramm; a "Bagatelle and Scherzo," for cello, performed at a benefit concert at which he was soloist; a Suite for the same instrument, given by the Symphony Society under Walter Damrosch; a male chorus, "Lied eines fahrenden Gesellen," sung by the Brooklyn Mannerchor at a private concert on April 6, 1890, and at which Mrs. Herbert made one of her rare public appearances after she had retired from the Metropolitan, singing, "Plus grand dans son obscurite," by Gounod; and the first cello concerto, of which Krehbiel was more critical than of Herbert's other early works. This was performed at a Philharmonic Young People's matinee, on December 10, 1887, a year after Herbert's arrival in New York, the conductor being Theodore Thomas. Krehbiel's opinion was:

"Victor Herbert's Concerto for violincello, played by the composer, was received with considerable favor. Here is a young musician (a grandson of Samuel Lover, by the way), an Irishman transformed into a German by education, who tried to escape the embarrassment caused by the dearth of solo music for his instrument by composing his own. It is a little singular that by so doing he comes dangerously near writing music that is beyond his powers of execution. It seemed as if he had done so yesterday, but it is possible he was not up to his usual standard as executant. His A string snarled nasally at times and his style had not the wholesome dignity and firmness that we have admired heretofore. It is neither meretricious nor commonplace. Only the orchestra part is treated a little too dryly."

The *World* critic differed from Krehbiel, as critics generally differ. He wrote:

"Victor Herbert, the cellist, came forward as a composer and soloist and in both showed his ability as an artist. His work, a Concerto for violincello, presented extreme difficulties for the solo instrument. This Mr. Herbert played with rare skill and finish; his tone is mellow and sympathetic and his playing of his own composition gave such pleasure to the audience that he was twice recalled. Mr. Herbert's genial presence makes itself felt alike to audience and orchestra."

But all this creative output had not meant much to Herbert except to increase his reputation as a fine, versatile musician. That was not entirely the reputation he wanted.

Often he said to Burck and to his other friends: "I wish I had a good comic opera libretto."

Operetta composition was clearly dominating his mind. And very properly. Herbert was entirely unfitted by temperament for serious music. He had little of that basic substance which was so prominently present in even the lightest and most melodious of the great composers, Mozart and Schubert.

Herbert, however, secretly compared himself to Schubert. He was like him in his facility for shaking out tunes any time and anywhere. But Herbert never had those hours of introspection, of pathos, of feeling for the world's undercurrents that were part of the life of Franz Schubert. Herbert could skim gayly, if vigorously, on the surface, but never could he go to any depths.

His career duplicates that of other composers of light music: Sullivan tried, before and after his operetta successes, to write serious music, but most of it failed. Offenbach is remembered entirely for his operettas. His "Tales of Hoffman," classed as grand opera, is really an elaborate operetta with a few dramatic scenes. Reginald de Koven, who wrote a good deal of serious music, is known only for his "Robin Hood," a comic opera.

Genius is necessary for the composition of good, light music; but it is a genius that cannot embrace all music.

Herbert's first association with music for the theater came in 1893, when he was commissioned to write portions of a great theatrical enterprise which Steele Mackaye was preparing as one of the attractions for the Chicago World's Fair. It was to be a great spectacle of the finding of America, housed in a huge auditorium built for such productions, called the "Spectatorium." The production was to be known as "Spectatorio," a word combined from "spectacle" and "oratorio," and Mackaye's idea was to go beyond Wagner in the combination of acting, music and scenery—to evolve a theatrical-musical presentation of a theme on an immense scale of realism.

A fortune was sunk in the enterprise, which remained unrealized. To-day it is memorable in stage history only for the numerous innovations Mackaye designed for it, and for the notable imagination which went into its planning.

Other parts of the music were written by Dvorák and an orchestra of one hundred and twenty men was to have been conducted by Seidl. Mackaye's son, Percy, the playwright and poet, says that portions of "The New World Symphony" went into Dvorák's music for his father's production.

As Mackaye was in Chicago, the negotiations with Herbert were conducted by his son, who wrote in his diary of March 18, 1893:

"Mother and I called on Mr. Victor Herbert, the

well-known cellist, who is writing the pantomimic music for the Spectatorium. He played some of the music, which is very fine. He lives at 1126 Park Avenue."

And in his history of his father's life, Percy Mackaye has these recollections:

"I remember vividly my conference at that time with the young, slim, black-haired celloist who was afterwards to become America's most popular composer. I remember his zest in playing 'pantomimic music' for my father's Spectatorio and the picturesque quality of his compositions. Twenty-three years later (January 19, 1916) when I had written him concerning a proposed meeting in memory of my father, he wrote me:

" 'Having known your dear father very well indeed, I consider it a great honor to have my name added to those of the committee.'

"Eight years afterwards, at lunch with him in the Lambs Club, I recalled our earliest work together, in which he had also set a choral song or two of mine to music for the Spectatorium; and he exclaimed: 'I am going to write you a tribute of my heart to your father's genius. I am rushed now, but I'll mail it to you within three weeks.' Within those three weeks, however, he had died, and a great outpouring of popular affection expressed itself at his funeral."

Mackaye's remembrance of Herbert in 1893 as "slim" is a deception of distance. He was always weighty.

The only benefit Herbert derived from his association with the Spectatorium was that he was brought closer to the stage. Soon afterwards he found the libretto for which he had been looking, and wrote his first produced comic opera, "Prince Ananias."

In testimony he gave at a court action some years later, Herbert referred to a first operetta that had not been produced. But there is no record of when it was written.

IX

"PRINCE ANANIAS" was produced by the Bostonians, and thus Victor Herbert came in contact with the most celebrated comic opera troupe this country has produced.

Many famous names are historically bound up with it, but at this distance three stand out: Reginald de Koven, Victor Herbert and Alice Nielsen. De Koven contributed "Robin Hood" to the Bostonians, Herbert "The Serenade" and Alice Nielsen her art as an operetta prima donna.

In the field of American music there never have been pieces so popular and worthy as "Robin Hood" and "The Serenade," or a singing actress, outside of grand opera, to achieve the fame of Alice Nielsen.

"The Bostonians" were organized in 1879 in an impromptu manner. The manager of the Boston Theatre, in Boston, needed a quick production to fill a hole in his schedule and decided to put on Gilbert and Sullivan's "Pinafore," with what he considered an ideal cast. With the help of a local concert manageress, Miss E. H. Ober, a company was assembled. These were the leading artists:

Adelaide Phillips, contralto; Myron W. Whitney, bass; Tom Karl, tenor; Henry Clay Barnabee, chief singing comedian; George B. Frothingham, a former minstrel; Arthur B. Hitchcock, baritone, and Georgia Cayvan, principally known as an elocutionist, who was later to be Daniel Frohman's famous leading lady of the Lyceum Stock Company.

They were all fine performers and merited the designation, "ideal cast," so much that they were called the Boston Ideal Opera Company. Just before the opening, Miss Phillips became ill and her place in "Pinafore" was taken by Mary Beebe, a young singer in whom Annie Louise Cary was interested.

"Pinafore" was a great success and after running nine weeks it was succeeded by "Fatinitza." The Boston Ideals were definitely launched.

Miss Ober was the directing head for six years, and the Ideals sported along in musical amusements like a large, happy family, having a good time themselves and giving the public competent and spirited performances of new and old operettas and the lighter grand operas. Then Miss Ober's place was taken by the company's advance agent, W. H. Foster, known more familiarly as "Colonel" Foster. He added some new singers, prominent among them Zelie de Lussan and Madame Lablache, a daughter of the noted singer of that name.

The engagement of the European diva was arranged by cable and was notable for an interchange of interesting messages. Madame Lablache cabled: "How shall I get to America? Collect." And Foster, who was economical, replied: "Swim. Collect."

The new manager adopted policies not too successful,

and two seasons later the company was reorganized by Barnabee, Karl, and W. H. McDonald, another member of the troupe, under a new name, "The Bostonians." This was the company that achieved the greatest renown of its tripartite history.

In 1890, "The Bostonians" tried out "Don Quixote," a piece written by two ambitious young men, Harry B. Smith and Reginald de Koven. It was their second collaboration. The first, "The Begum," was a moderate success. "Don Quixote," though, was a complete failure. To make amends, they shortly after sent Barnabee—"Barney," for all purposes but the record— a manuscript entitled, "Robin Hood."

"Oh, Promise Me," our national wedding institution, was not in the original production of "Robin Hood." It was interpolated in the English version and later arranged for Jessie Bartlett Davis, one of the most popular members of the troupe, who made a personal hit with it.

"Robin Hood" was given its première in 1890, in Chicago. Thereafter, it became the dearest hope of the Bostonians to find a successor to this gold mine. One did not appear until seven years later, when Victor Herbert and "Robin Hood's" librettist created "The Serenade." In 1894, however, the company had an unsuspected premonition of the joys to come in "Prince Ananias."

Herbert had found a gentleman named Francis Nielsen who provided him with a satirical libretto a good deal in the Gilbertian style. It was partly Mr.

Nielsen's intention to rub it into certain types of stage
folk as Shakespeare had done in "A Midsummer Night's
Dream." But while all agreed that it was an unusual
libretto and that the score was attractive and more
musicianly and ambitious than most musical productions of the time, "Prince Ananias" was a failure.

It was produced at the Broadway Theatre, New
York, on November 20, 1894. The story is that of a
romantic and sentimental outlaw, a vagabond poet, a
band of strolling players, an actress who had married
three nobles and entered into a contract with her manager to avoid marriage for five years—thereby antici-
pating the modern Hollywood pacts—and a jilted
heroine.

It opens encouragingly enough with a chorus by
villagers who announce joyously that Ninette, who has
"jilted swains of every size," is about to rope in the
local miser. Ninette then sings a song of crocodilean
sorrow:

"A dutious wife I soon shall be,
    For to-morrow at the altar
The priest will give a man to me,
With him to live, with him agree,
    And promise make to be his slave—
    I almost quake, no power to save.
What shall I do? Oh, dear, dear me,
    Now I think I'm going to falter.

"A maid is rash, a fool is she,
    Once it's done she cannot alter;
The priest can't give you back the youth
You once did live, it is the truth;

Henceforth you weep and mend and bake,
And vigils keep—for mercy's sake
What shall I do? Oh, dear, dear me,
Now I'm sure I'm going to falter."

Later the manager of the strolling players enters on a donkey and in response to applause makes this speech:

"Ladies and Gentlemen: This jovial reception has caused every emotion in me to tingle with unadulterated pleasure. Although I have been enthusiastically received in all the principal one-night stands throughout this glorious country, I must confess I've never been so moved before—" (here the donkey bucks, with damage to the manager's dignity).

He then sings:

"An author-manager am I
Of a company artistic;
Some say the apple of my eye
Is the ultra-realistic!
I try to humor every class,
For which the press say I'm an ass.
The compliment I oft return,
In language hot enough to burn,
But phœnix-like they seem to be
Whenever a play's produced by me.
If I did not to plays give birth
There'd be no critics on the earth."

It was all done with a laudable purpose, but Nielsen was no Gilbert, and Herbert an amateur at satire. Barnabee at first had sufficient faith in "Prince Ananias" to alternate it with "Robin Hood" on a road tour, but soon abandoned it.

This failure, however, was to result in profits, though not for Barney and his colleagues. At the time of its production, Kirke La Shelle, a former Chicago newspaper man, was the business manager for the Bostonians. There was a quarrel and La Shelle left, after first providing himself with a substitute activity in the management of Frank Daniels. Daniels was the only actor in a family of dentists, had lived in Boston, played there in comic opera and was beginning to establish a reputation as a comedian.

In the summer of 1895, La Shelle was a neighbor of Harry B. Smith at a New Jersey vacation resort. He was hunting a vehicle for Daniels, and Smith offered him a story which both La Shelle and Daniels liked. It came to a question as to who was to compose the music. La Shelle remembered Herbert and suggested him. He had recognized in this musician with a classical background and the heart of an actor a promising possibility for the operetta stage.

Neither Smith, Daniels nor La Shelle's partner, Arthur Clark, took to the idea of entrusting their future to the author of a failure, but La Shelle insisted. He asked Smith at least to finish an act of the book and permit Herbert to have a try at it.

Smith agreed, and so eager was Herbert to dip again into operetta that he had the first act ready in two weeks after he received the manuscript. All concerned went over to Herbert's home where he played the music. They found it good, though Smith observes that "it was rather obscured by Herbert's piano play-ing."

This piece was "The Wizard of the Nile," Herbert's first successful operetta. It was produced, after a few weeks' trial out of town, at the Casino Theatre in New York, on November 4, 1895.

Herbert wrote this score at great speed and did not spare himself. Most of it was composed while he was playing an engagement with Gilmore's Band at the Atlanta, Georgia, exposition, and every spare hour went into the "Wizard." Otto Schreiber, the bandsman, tells how, one night, after the concert, he came into Herbert's quarters in the exposition building and found him half naked, sweltering in the heat, but driving away without interruption at the score.

"You will kill yourself with work," Schreiber said, awed by such industry. Herbert laughed him away.

Schreiber is of the opinion, based on his lengthy experience with Herbert, that he generally composed away from the piano and that he never revised. He does not know of a single instance where a change in Herbert's music was made by the composer.

Although Smith has written so many librettos that even he has lost count, "The Wizard of the Nile," produced so long ago, is one of his best. It has a burlesque story of Egypt when Cleopatra was a young girl and details the adventures of a wandering faker named "Kibosh" who strolls into the land of the Pharaoh Ptolemy just after His Majesty had invested all his surplus cash in desert property, trusting to the

Anton Seidl with Mrs. Seidl.

A Snapshot of Victor Herbert in the Adirondacks.
His Arm Is Around His Son, Clifford.

prophecy of his weather man that heavy floods would cover the waste land. The rains have failed to materialize and the weather prophet is about to be beheaded. In this situation Kibosh becomes involved, with all sorts of opportunities for comedy.

Daniels was ideal for the part and made the most of it. He originated a bit of colloquialism that is in use to this day. A catch line of the piece was "Am I a wizard!" Daniels abbreviated this boast into "Am I a wiz!" And "wiz" is now included in the dictionary of Americanisms.

Later on the comedian was fond of telling this story, which had its basis in "The Wizard of the Nile":

"One of Kibosh's pieces of stage business was the extraction of eggs from the mouths of various characters. I would pat the person on the head, wave my hand and extract an egg from the mouth, remarking as I did it: 'Am I a wiz?' Some years later, Charlie Dillingham presented me with a fine English bulldog. I put him in my country place at Rye, New York, and from then on I began to notice that the supply of eggs from our hennery was diminishing. One afternoon I was walking about the grounds when I noticed the dog acting in a suspicious way near the hennery. I called to him and he waddled over with a guilty look. I talked to him and encouragingly patted his head. To my surprise an egg rolled out of his mouth, bringing back to me the days of my wizardry."

Smith was to compose fourteen operettas with Herbert, but he was more of a work-mate than the boon

companion that Herbert liked to make of his close
colleagues. The librettist is the reverse of the public's
conception of a comic writer. He is a grave-faced
gentleman—now in his late sixties—with a scholarly
mind and a passion for collecting rare books and manuscripts.

His home in New York is the sort of warmly dignified old mansion that one associates with a literary
English baronet. His chief interest is in writing essays
on Dickens and other classical authors, and for some
time past he has been writing about his researches in
Napoleonic data. One of his most valued possessions
is the lengthy appeal Napoleon dictated to a secretary
on St. Helena.

Outside of his Irish compatriots—to whom he was
bound by emotions—Herbert had few friends of this
type. Although he and Smith lived within a few blocks
of each other, they rarely visited except to work, and
then they were so absorbed in what they were doing
that they paid little attention to one another.

Smith retains some interesting recollections of Herbert. Herbert and de Koven, he says, were not the
best of friends. De Koven was particularly offended
with Herbert because the latter had branded one of his
works as "rubbish." He was offended, too, on one
occasion with Smith because he stated in an article that
Herbert was the "most versatile musician in America."
Smith's reason for this declaration was that no other
musician in this country covered such a wide field in
music.

The librettist recalls that Victor Herbert was very critical of other composers' works. He could find little value in Grieg, and derided Puccini's "Madame Butterfly." Schubert, on the other hand, was his ideal, and he observed that "not one note of his songs can be changed." He similarly idolized Wagner and once, when a pianist had finished playing a transcription of "Tristan und Isolde," he exclaimed to Smith: "That is the finest music in the world!"

He admired Tschaikovsky. Herbert once took Smith to hear the Russian conductor, Safonov, direct the Philharmonic at Carnegie Hall in Tschaikovsky's "Pathetique" symphony. Herbert was depressingly affected by the music and later, when the critic, Krehbiel, had joined them, they walked into a neighboring saloon and discussed the concert.

"It is magnificent music," said Herbert, "but I wish it had never been written."

Incidentally, Smith relates that when he asked Krehbiel on that occasion which Wagnerian opera he thought would endure the longest, the critic replied "Faust."

While Herbert was critical of established composers he was very tolerant of beginners, Smith declares, and relates an instance of a well-known comedian who had taken to writing serious music. He produced a Mass, and when he took it to a publisher's office he found Herbert there. Herbert was asked for his opinion. He opened the expensively bound manuscript, which was titled auspiciously, "Grand Mass in F," read a number of pages, and commented: "By Jove, it *is* in F!"

Probably Smith's memory lapsed in this case. Herbert would have found it as difficult to utter the English, "By Jove!" as an Englishman to eat frogs' legs.

The success of "The Wizard of the Nile" was more the success of Daniels and the book than the music. The score has a few attractive numbers, a few effective concerted pieces, but much commonplace and reminiscent writing. Its main virtue is a workmanlike finish. One can see that here is a man who has a perfect control over all the elements he handles; the orchestra, the chorus, the solo, the adaption of music to actions are all as they should be. There is not a trace of the slipshod, ragged writing musical comedies on Broadway were—and are—accustomed to. It is not such good comic opera, but it is comic opera a producer can approach with the confidence that it will give satisfaction.

For a second effort it showed a grasp of operetta technique that established Herbert as instinctively suited for that work. A man to whom this medium would not be the most natural one would have had more difficulties with it.

The Herbert idiosyncrasy of injecting difficult intervals in his songs shows itself prominently in "The Wizard of the Nile." Abrupt jumps of fourths, fifths, sixths are common, while in the main waltz song—a banal thing—there is a jump of a ninth, from the low D to the high F.

"The Wizard of the Nile" was translated into German under the title, "Der Zauberer vom Nil," and produced in that language both here—at the Terrace

Garden, New York, May 20, 1897—and probably in Vienna, where it was published by the State publishing house.

With the success of this piece came a commission from the Bostonians to write an operetta. In his book, "My Wanderings," Henry Clay Barnabee records this event thus:

"We were now searching diligently for another 'Robin Hood' and allusions to such a find occasionally permeated our thought-cells. A number of authors and composers, besides the original pair, enthusiastically shouted, 'Eureka!' But the vast majority of the people in the seats silently but none the less effectively responded: 'Come off your perch!'

"Nevertheless we did strike it. It was 'The Serenade.' In this delightful creation Messrs. Herbert and Smith handed us out an artistic financial atonement for the four-flushing 'Knickerbockers', by Smith and Henry Waller, and the false-throated 'Prince Ananias,' in what I regard as the best American contribution to genuine comic opera—as distinguished from musical comedy, which I consider 'Robin Hood' to be—up to now revealed.

" 'The Serenade' furnished a spanking vehicle for the various talents of the company. The public agreed with our estimate this time and we enjoyed five more 'fat' years with the repertoire thus strengthened."

Before going on further with this episode in Herbert's career—one of the most important, for it is on "The Serenade" that much of his fame is built—it is well to interpolate a sketch written by Eugene Cowles, the Bostonians' popular baritone, of Barnabee, the man who is directly responsible for "The Serenade," and a notable figure in the history of comic opera in this country. The sketch was written when "Barney" was in his last years and the Bostonians had been disrupted and disbanded in poverty.

"I was a member of the organization for ten years and can safely say that I know Mr. Barnabee as well as any man living knows him. He is a man of rugged honesty, peculiar temper and temperament, kind-hearted and generous to a fault; as alive to what is going on in the world at seventy-seven as he was twenty years ago, and in spite of physical disability caused by two serious accidents, which would have placed any one with a less rugged constitution and a feebler will in an invalid chair or on crutches.

"Mr. Barnabee has been blamed, as were the owners of the Bostonians, for not accumulating a large 'nest-egg' in the time of their wonderful prosperity, and the fact that they did not must seem strange and almost unpardonable to many. However, I think I can explain in a great measure their failure to do so, and in speaking of the acts of the Bostonians I am referring to the policy of Mr. Barnabee, for he was always the senior manager.

"First: They were the first managers to give encouragement to native composers, and always had faith in them; so that while they had two successes, 'Robin Hood' and 'The Serenade,' they put on many pieces by American composers which were absolute failures, and any one who knows the theatrical business can give you an idea of how much may be lost on a comic opera production which falls short of success.

"Second: They were extremely generous, not only to personal friends, but to members of the theatrical profession. I know of cases where they provided backing for young actors who appeared in the galaxy of stars and who failed, perhaps through no fault of their own. On more than one occasion they returned entire companies to New York from San Francisco. These companies were stranded; closed in San Francisco by unscrupulous Eastern managers. Without saying anything, even to the members of their own company Barnabee and his partners paid railroad fares for the stranded actors and sent them to New York.

"Third: I was in the company during the disastrous season of 1893-4 when the theatrical business was at a low ebb and cash a scarcity. Yet Mr. Barnabee never allowed a Saturday to go by with a single salary unpaid, even if he was forced to borrow money on personal collateral to fill out the pay roll.

"Fourth: They never gave any one a two-weeks' notice. In the cases of numerous singers engaged at the opening of the season who failed to make good, the management carried them uncomplainingly all the season from Maine to California and back, and handed them their envelopes every Saturday until summer (or death) released them.

"These are some of the reasons why money did not stick to Henry Clay Barnabee, and while these reasons would probably be ridiculed by the theatre managers of to-day they are to me evidence of his kind heart and Americanism.

"Professionally Mr. Barnabee was in a class by himself; it seems to me his chief hold upon the audiences was due to his clear-cut enunciation. Every syllable of song or dialogue was crisp and distinct. To this he added an unctuous physiognomy and the keenest sense of humor. This sense of humor helped him through many annoyances and now it enables him to face old age and infirmity with serenity."

The Bostonians disbanded in the twenty-fifth year of their illustrious existence. Defections, changes, lack of good new material, added to the reasons given by Cowles, brought about the end. An anonymous piece called, "The Queen of Laughter," served as their incongruous swan song. Barney described the end with poignant feeling:

"At Atlantic City, New Jersey, by the sad sea waves, on Young's Pier, with a ten-cent audience in the rear looking coldly on, the 'Queen of Laughter' smiled her last and the proud Bostonians went down, with the colors of their long and valiant career still flying.

"Yes, the end had come! The last ripple of applause had been washed up by the sea—the last chord of music had sounded—the last note sung—the last curtain drawn—the last light out—the last exit at the back of the gilded sphere—

"Words are useless, vain! History and memory

must comfort the mourner as well as serve the preacher. That's all that's left."

In the midst of paying off debts and settling himself into what was for him a new life, the ligaments of one of Barney's knees snapped and when he recovered, after spending several months on a stretcher, he was given two great benefits, one in New York and the other in Boston. These served as the climax to his career. At the New York benefit, Herbert came to the assistance of his old mentor and helped to make it an enormous success. The *Herald* reported this closing chapter with interesting details:

"One of the largest audiences ever crowded into the Broadway Theatre attended the testimonial performance given yesterday afternoon (May 11, 1906), under the auspices of the Lambs Club, for Mr. Henry Clay Barnabee and Mrs. William H. McDonald (his late partner's widow), former members of the Bostonians. The total receipts were more than $22,000, which did not include the cancellation of notes given by Mr. Barnabee to friends for $10,000, which were destroyed in favor of the actor when it became known that he was in financial difficulties. One of these notes was held by the late Senator M. A. Hanna, and when he died it was left to his widow. When Mrs. Hanna learned that Mr. Barnabee was to have a benefit, she sent word to the men in charge of the testimonial that she had destroyed the note of the actor, as did two other persons who held Mr. Barnabee's paper for $5,000. These notes were secured by life insurance held by the aged actor, and by their holders giving them up they as much as presented Mr. Barnabee with $10,000.

"Mr. Barnabee himself appeared upon the stage and read an elegant and touching appreciation on behalf of himself and Mrs. McDonald of the kindness of all who had assisted in the benefit. At the end the aged actor and singer broke down and wept."

Herbert's contribution to the program was a specially arranged fantasie of "The Serenade," which was played by his orchestra.

Barnabee was one of the pioneers of American music. He loved the operetta, considered it an art, and gave himself to its advancement with all his heart. There are few like him to-day, when a musical production—any stage production, in fact—is either a success or a "flop."

"The Serenade" had a clever plot by Harry B. Smith.

A song—the serenade of the title—is sung by a Spanish lover to his lady, the ward of an eccentric old noble who wants to marry her. The old gentleman endeavors to discover the identity of the love thief by this song, which crops up in many places, sung by different people. It is an ideal plot for an operetta, since the action grows out of the music itself. Herbert made the most of it.

The serenade itself is one of the most charming melodies to be found in all his scores, as is also the waltz song, "Cupid and I." This song was not originally a part of the score. It was written for the use of Dorothy Morton, a comic opera singer of that period who is reputed to have had a beautiful coloratura voice. For some reason Miss Morton did not accept it—to her great regret later—and when Alice Nielsen was given the rôle of "Yvonne," Herbert interpolated this song for her. During a rehearsal one afternoon he decided that Miss Nielsen should have a cadenza for this number and in his usual impulsive manner sat down at the piano and dashed it off. Miss Nielsen sang it directly afterward and it remained permanently in the score.

It is not, however, that the score of "The Serenade" is so overflowing with distinctive melodies as that the music generally is good and effective. As Barnabee said, it is true operetta, a genuine work of its kind in all respects.

It was first produced in Chicago, and shortly after opened at the Knickerbocker Theatre, New York, on March 16, 1897.

It was liked at once. Krehbiel gave it one of his scholarly reviews:

"Clever conceits, which work out well when mixed with operetta are not so many that a librettist should despise them because they have served their purpose once, or even oftener. A single theme has done duty in the modern French drama for decades and there is no indication that the end is near. So Mr. Harry B. Smith deserves to be praised rather than faulted for his choice of an old idea as the foundation for an operetta called 'The Serenade.' . . . A note on the house bill credited 'the theme' to Goldoni, a source which no librettist need hesitate to confess; but we fancy the Italian classic reached Mr. Smith through a French filter, and it will not wrench even a weak memory to recall that one of the dramatic notions in the piece—that of a person who is a bandit and monk on alternate days—was ingeniously exploited by Mr. Gilbert in 'The Mountebank.' . . .

"Herbert has handled this element with real ingenuity. His travesty of a singing lesson, beginning with exercises in *mezzo di voce* is most excellent musical fooling; a waltz song in the second act, written for the soprano of the company, is charming, though not strikingly original; a Spanish dance which occurs early in the same act, and which is utilized in the finale, is as bright and effective as Sir Arthur Sullivan's 'Cachuca' in 'The Gondoliers,' and an Angelus song for contralto and chorus, with obligato bell chimes is decidedly ambitious in its structure and admirable.

"The operetta achieved a decided success, which was weakened only by the too great anxiety of Mr. Herbert, who conducted the music of the performance, to repeat the most popular numbers. As a consequence the audience left the theater thoroughly weary half an hour before midnight.

"At the end of the second act librettist and composer joined the company on the stage and Mr. Barnabee, Mr. Smith and Mr. Herbert told the audience how grateful they were to the dear public and how much they admired each other. One of Mr. Smith's remarks was not only a wise observation, but one which it was safe to venture in the presence of the many indications which the evening afforded that 'The Serenade' is bound to be more than ordinarily successful. He gave it as his observation that when a comic opera succeeds the people say: 'What beautiful music!' and when it fails: 'What a bad book!'"

The axiom which Smith introduced in that curtain speech was born out of much vexation. Librettists always have an ungrateful job. Whether their books are good or bad they remain largely unknown to the public, and if the production fails, they are most often blamed, if not by the indifferent public, at least by the composer and producer.

Smith, in fact, has good cause for complaint in his association with Herbert. It has been a standing criticism of the latter that he usually consented to work with librettists who were not of his standard, and that if he had had a Gilbert for his partner his works would have been on a higher shelf in the archives of posterity. That is obviously an unreasonable criticism, for Herbert was a romanticist and not a satirist, and Gilbert would have been as handicapped by Herbert as the composer by him.

Apart from that, subtle intellectuality was never a trait of Herbert's, and Gilbert would have had little patience with him. The librettos Herbert got were, generally, very suitable to his temperament and style.

In the review quoted above, the erudite Krehbiel made what is known as a bloomer. He suggested that

[117]

Smith got his idea for "The Serenade" from a French dramatist, instead of from the Italian, Goldoni. The fact is the story was original with Smith.

Some time before "The Serenade" was produced, an operetta by Richard Genee, called "Nanon," was playing at the Casino. It had a musical theme which recurred throughout the piece but which had no reference to the action. Smith was afraid that he would be accused of borrowing from "Nanon" and to avoid this he inserted in the program of "The Serenade" the note: "The plot was derived from an interlude by Goldoni." Of course Goldoni had written no such interlude.

Nevertheless, Smith could not prevent a comparison with "Nanon" in the press. In the *World* review, there was the following:

"The music is modern throughout. Its type is Viennese. Genee, of 'Nanon' fame, is one of the models, but there are deft hints of the better class of music-hall ditties—the *Ca fait toujours plaisir* of Yvette Gilbert is one—which gives it the note of actuality."

This critic was most enthusiastic about "The Serenade." A few more comic operas with as virile, vivacious and versatile a score, he said, "and America will then be the purveyor of light, humorous and sprightly music to the theaters of Europe. The debt incurred by the reception of the work by Offenbach, Lecocq, Planquette, Suppe and Sullivan will be liquidated by the gift of scores of Edwards, Sousa, Englander and Herbert."

There was irony in the fact that "The Serenade"

review in the *World* was followed by a review of Mozart's "The Magic Flute" at the Metropolitan Opera House, signed by Reginald de Koven.

In this out-of-the-way detail can be found a good basis for the comparison between the two men which is often made. Herbert could never have written a criticism of "The Magic Flute," even though he was able to express himself well in writing.

Krehbiel's comment on Herbert's anxiety to repeat the most popular numbers from "The Serenade" strikes on the composer's major characteristic. It was always mainly the audience with Herbert, and he gloried in its applause.

Harry Somers, who used to be the manager of the Knickerbocker Theatre in New York, where a number of the Herbert operettas were produced, says that when Herbert conducted at the opening nights or on other important occasions, he used to send the conductor out to the orchestra through the back of the house and down the center aisle, at the same time playing the spotlight on his commanding figure. Herbert, Somers said, used to take the greatest delight in this maneuver, bowing and smiling happily as he advanced to the pit.

"The Serenade" introduced Alice Nielsen as a prima donna, the singer who became so notably identified with Herbert's music. Barnabee found her singing with a light opera stock company in San Francisco.

"In Frisco," Barnabee said, "we struck 'pay dirt' in the discovery of Alice Nielsen. She was obscured in the Tivoli company, but her fresh young voice, sympathetic face and vivacious personality could not long remain hidden anywhere."

And "pay dirt" Alice was for the Bostonians, as long as she remained with them. She emerged as one of the best sopranos in the country. She was blessed additionally with a good figure, a handsome face, vivaciousness and acting talent.

Miss Nielsen was born in Nashville, Tennessee. Her father was Erasmus Ivarius Nielsen, a painter. After he died of wounds received as a Union soldier in the Civil War, the mother and seven children moved to Kansas City where Mrs. Nielsen kept a boarding house.

In those days the future internationally-famous diva ran about the streets of Kansas City barefoot and in a torn dress. Something different about her made the boys of her neighborhood—Twelfth and Locusts streets —tease her. She achieved her first hit by cracking an egg over the head of one of her tormenters.

She joined a church choir, and whatever she knew of music and voice culture—save for a few random lessons from a Kansas City teacher named Desci—she picked up there, and at amateur theatrical productions and concerts at which she sang. So poor was she that she appeared on the platform time and again in the same dress of cheap material.

She married the organist of the church, Benjamin Nentwig (against her mother's wishes—Mrs. Nielsen would not go to the wedding) and embarked upon a period of discordant matrimony. Eventually the couple were divorced and Alice went to San Francisco with her brother.

When she sang at a mass in St. Patrick's church, the beauty of her voice attracted attention and she was given other church engagements. An appearance at the Orpheum followed, and then she went into the Tivoli Theatre, where she became a favorite.

Alice Nielsen's first theatrical appearance actually took place in Kansas City when she was eight, but no one saw her performance. Always dreaming of opera, she stole into the Coates Opera House during an engagement of an opera troupe and curled into a throne which stood back stage. From that secret position she heard "The Bohemian Girl"—by coincidence the opera by Balfe, Samuel Lover's friend—and was properly thrilled. After the audience, singers and stage crew left the theater, she crept out of the chair. A single bunch-light threw a dim light into the auditorium.

Alice walked hesitantly to the center of the stage and stood fascinated. An entrancing picture swept into her mind of a great audience listening breathlessly to her singing, and caused her to open her mouth and send a ringing: "I Dreamt I Dwelt in Marble Halls" into the empty theater.

As she finished and bowed gravely, the bunch-light went out and left her in ghostly darkness. Wild screams succeeded Balfe's aria and the box-office man found her later in hysterics.

After Barnabee took her with him she appeared in the repertoire of the Bostonians. During rehearsals of

"The Serenade," the company was playing at the old Murray Hill Theatre in New York in "A War Time Wedding," a musical fantasia by Oscar Weil, known originally as "In Mexico." According to Miss Nielsen's story, it was while she was in that cast that Mrs. Herbert heard her, was attracted by her voice and ability, and advised Herbert to give her the leading rôle of "Yvonne" in the new operetta. Herbert, Miss Nielsen says, took his wife's advice to the extent of coming to hear her. He was similarly attracted and asked McDonald, partner with Barnabee in the ownership of the Bostonians, to try her out in the part.

"Yvonne" had been assigned to Hilda Clark, a stately blonde beauty very popular with audiences, and he refused. But Herbert insisted, and at the next rehearsal Miss Nielsen was asked to do a number from "The Serenade."

Miss Clark had interpreted "Yvonne" in rather a serious manner; Alice gave it dash of burlesque and jollity. Besides, she could dance, and Miss Clark couldn't. Herbert was highly pleased, but McDonald still wanted Miss Clark.

Thereupon Herbert picked up his score and said, in effect: "No Nielsen; no 'Serenade!'" A compromise was eventually reached which provided for the two sopranos alternating the part.

Herbert now found himself thoroughly launched on his new career. Daniels needed a new vehicle, and so the authors of "The Wizard of the Nile" got up another piece called, "The Idol's Eye." This was produced at the Broadway Theatre, October 25, 1897, and was also successful.

Like the other work, much of its popularity must be put down to the humor of Daniels and the novelty of the book. Smith dug down into Eastern lore again and uncovered a legendary law which made the man who rescued a suicide responsible for all the latter's actions, past and present. The hero of "The Idol's Eye" rescues a tramp Scotchman from self-extinction in India, and thus becomes his surety. When McSnuffy reveals himself to be a kleptomaniac and the rash person who stole the sacred idol's ruby eye, the comic complications are obvious.

As in "The Wizard of the Nile," Daniels had one of the best songs, "The Tattooed Man." The lyric had a clever circus idea:

"Do you remember, Angeline,
    That heartless 'Human Snake'?
Who won my heart, in another part,
    And gave that heart a break?
I'll sing you now of my sweet revenge,
    'Twas retribution stern;
She fell in love with a tattooed man,
    Who broke her heart in turn.

CHORUS

"He was such a human picture gallery,
    Such a spectacular gent;
He won her heart and drew her salary,
    He never gave a cent.
Till one good day, with her season's pay
    And the Fat Lady off he ran,

Oh, 'tis perfectly true, you can beat a tattoo,
But you can't beat a tattooed man.

"He had designs upon himself,
    She had designs on him;
She loved to look at the picture book
    He had on every limb;
'Oh, why should I go abroad?' she said,
    'To Germany, France or Rome,
'With a lovely collection, awaiting inspection,
    'In my happy little home?'

CHORUS

"He'd Raphael's Cherubs on his brow,
    The Angelus on his chest;
While on his back, was a liberal stack,
    Of Old Masters of the best.
'Oh, picture to yourself,' she said,
    'A lovelorn maiden's doom.'
'I cannot picture to myself,' he said,
    'For there's no more room.'"

The human picture gallery idea has been used in varied forms since "The Idol's Eye." The last transformation can be seen to-day as a burlesque stock bit, in which the anatomical illustrations are not quite so æsthetic as Smith made them.

For the music of this operetta, not much enthusiasm can be worked up. A criticism which appeared in *Plays and Players*, following the première, fairly describes it:

"The music of this opera is what we have learned to expect from Victor Herbert—upon one hand, not trashy; upon the other, not strikingly original.

[124]

"The first half hour of the music is the most entertaining. It contains a balloon song—an engaging bit of melody, and the entrance song of the Cuban. The accompaniment of this song and the succeeding chorus is the freshest and most ingeniously conceived bit of harmony in the opera.

"There is a concerted piece in the minor full of excellent modulations not usual in light opera, but in no way new to music. The coon song clings to one's memory and so does 'The Tattooed Man.' But on the whole the music, though not tedious, will hardly be immortal."

Herbert seemed too much influenced by the job of creating a vehicle for an extravaganza comedian to feel himself free to write as he might have wished.

X

VICTOR HERBERT's versatility now enabled him to calmly make the jump from the buffoonery of "The Idol's Eye" to the serious business of conducting a symphony orchestra.

A few years before this, in 1895, Andrew Carnegie presented Pittsburgh with a library and music hall, thus providing an incentive for the establishment of a permanent symphonic organization. A cultured citizen named Charles W. Scovel, one of those local heroes who spend a lifetime in the artistic advancement of their city and remain unknown to the rest of the country, got together the subscriptions to guarantee the start of such an orchestra. He imported Frederick Archer, an eminent organist, as conductor and organist of the music hall. A year later, on February 27, 1896, the first concert of the Pittsburgh Symphony Orchestra was given.

Herbert was the next conductor, taking the post in 1898. For six years thereafter he divided his time between leading this orchestra and writing operettas and musical comedies. He did both with remarkable ease. No other person in the history of modern music ever demonstrated such a strange duality. Beethoven and ballads!

But he enjoyed his new work immensely and was proud of it.

"I am one of the few Irishmen," he used to say, "at the head of a great symphony orchestra."

The years he spent in Pittsburgh were among the happiest of his life. He came in contact on an equal basis with the many great figures in music who visited Pittsburgh, and they were all entertained royally at his home.

He lived comfortably, and his residence on Aikins Avenue was well furnished and had a good billiard room in the attic. Billiards was the only game Herbert really enjoyed.

When Richard Strauss came to Pittsburgh to conduct the orchestra in some of his own work, his wife, Pauline de Ahna, a singer and soloist at her husband's concerts, was greatly surprised as Mrs. Herbert showed her through the house. She could not understand how a mere conductor could afford such munificence and confessed that she, herself, had to be content with a much less pretentious home.

"To think—she has it all to herself!" she exclaimed, when she saw the array of fancy combs and other toilet articles on Mrs. Herbert's dresser.

One day some years ago, Henry Burck, the second concert master of the Pittsburgh orchestra, met Fritz Kreisler and the latter mourned:

"Where are those happy days at Pittsburgh!"

He recalled particularly, Burck said, one Sunday he

spent with Victor Herbert, after his Saturday appearance with the orchestra.

"That was the day," Burck said, "when we played the Schubert String Quintet three times.

"Herbert used to invite a number of the orchestra players to his home for Sunday, and with Kreisler there was also Von Kunitz, the concert master, Henry Merck, the first cellist, and myself. We came early and before dinner (lunch you would call it) it was suggested that we have an appetizer by playing the Schubert Quintet. Kreisler took the first violin part and Herbert the cello.

"It was a magnificent performance. Kreisler was enthusiastic. After we had finished, a grand dinner was served—such as Mrs. Herbert knew so well how to prepare. She was a noble cook, and when she did not herself do the cooking, she supervised the kitchen strictly.

"The dinner, after the quintet, left us in a warm and poetic mood. We had a few drinks and cigars and then Kreisler said: 'Let us play the quintet again.'

"So we took up our instruments and played once more. Again we were all in raptures. Herbert then led us up to the attic for billiards and a few more drinks. Supper followed, and before returning to the Stanley Hotel, where he was staying, Kreisler asked to play the quintet for the third time. We did—with the same pleasure as before.

"When we parted late that evening we had spent one of the most completely happy days of our musical lives."

Herbert's direction of the Pittsburgh Symphony Orchestra pleased his audiences, if it did not entirely satisfy the professional musicians and experienced concert-goers of the city.

The late Adolph M. Foerster, a well-known Pittsburgh composer and conductor, said of him:

"Possessing great familiarity with orchestral resources, and being a persevering worker, his influence exerted itself beneficially for the orchestra. Brilliancy and verve were the most promising characteristics of his work; sometimes, though, his exuberance seemed rather excessive; what often appeared an advantage in modern music proved a detriment in the classical. Mr. Herbert's advent was marked by virility and his programs were never tedious. During the greater part of his incumbency the orchestra consisted of sixty-five men."

The scope of Herbert's performances can be judged from this list of symphonies in the Pittsburgh orchestra's repertoire during his fourth season:

Beethoven . . . . . Sixth, Seventh and Eighth Symphonies.
Berlioz . . . . Symphonie Fantastique.
Brahms . . . . Second Symphony.
Dvorák . . . . New World.
Glazounoff . . . . . Sixth Symphony.
Hadley . . . . The Four Seasons.
Haydn . . . . Second and Seventeenth Symphonies.

Mozart .... G Minor.
Rubinstein ..... The Ocean.
Raff .... Lenore.
Saint-Saëns .... Third Symphony.
Schubert .... C Major.
Tschaikovsky ... Fifth and Manfred.

Of the miscellaneous music he favored the French composers. Berlioz, Chausson, Saint-Saëns, Delibes, D'Indy, Massenet, Franck, Dubois, Chabrier, Chaminade, Bizet were frequently heard at his concerts. Wagner was his standard composer.

He also took the opportunity to introduce his own "Suite for Strings," "Suite Romantique," "Hero and Leander," "Woodland Fancies" and the "Columbus Suite."

He built his programs in an individual manner and one which showed his strong sense of the theatre. The symphony was first, next came the suite, or numbers with a soloist, and lastly a group of light pieces.

"The best should come first," he said, "while the audience is still fresh."

Strauss was well pleased with Herbert's preparation of the orchestra for the three compositions he played with it: "Death and Transfiguration," "Till Eulenspiegel," and the love scene from the opera, "Feursnot."

They were first given in Cleveland, where Strauss was the guest conductor of the Pittsburgh band. He sent Herbert a telegram saying how much he admired his work. This message provided substantial comfort for Herbert whenever he felt hurt by criticisms which stressed his musical comedy side.

Later, when Strauss conducted in Pittsburgh, he was quite friendly with Herbert. Always ready for fun, Herbert had a picture taken of the orchestra with Strauss on the podium and himself behind a bass fiddle. Strauss matched him by having the photographer take another picture with Herbert as conductor and himself as the bass player. They interchanged these photographs as souvenirs.

During rehearsals for "Eulenspiegel," Herbert was delighted by the novel and modernistic effects Strauss obtained from the various instruments and was additionally pleased to taunt a conservative old player with the remark:

"How do you like it, Pop?"

Pop's reply was in variants of: "It ain't music!"— at which, "Herbert's belly used to shake with laughing," as one of his musicians put it.

Although he was so strict with his men at rehearsals, demanding a high level of performance and roundly cursing them when they failed to please him, there was always a good comradeship between them and himself. The serenades for his birthday continued as in the previous days with the band, and on every St. Patrick's Day every player appeared at rehearsals with a green necktie. Rehearsals were held daily. Among the orchestra's birthday gifts to Herbert was a loving cup with an Irish harp engraved on it, and a carved oaken dining-room table—both most appropriate.

Once there was a squabble in the orchestra which resulted in making public some of Herbert's characteristics as an orchestral trainer. In the middle of the 1903 season, the Pittsburgh Art Society, sponsors of the orchestra, received this letter from Gaston Borch, the second cellist:

"When I entered into correspondence with Mr. Hennenberg (who acted as business chief of the orchestra) regarding a position as cellist in the Pittsburgh Orchestra, I stated that I did not wish to come to Pittsburgh for a season of twenty weeks. Mr. Hennenberg, for Mr. Herbert, wrote me that I would have to play for Mr. Herbert before rehearsals began and he would then decide which place I was to have in the orchestra. I played for Mr. Herbert and he found me good enough to engage me as the second solo cellist and induced me to take that position, telling me it would mean a much longer engagement, as he was going to take part of the orchestra on a concert tour after the Pittsburgh season and I, as second cellist, would be sure to continue with him as long as the orchestra was together. These were the conditions on which I accepted the position as solo cellist.

"Since that time, Mr. Herbert, for personal reasons, has changed his mind and, without giving me any notice, has engaged another cellist to take my place for the spring tour. He has thus broken his engagement with me.

[132]

"Mr. Herbert treats the men of the orchestra in such a rough and vulgar way that the Art Society will find the orchestra less good every year, instead of improving, as no musician who is good enough to do something else would submit to Mr. Herbert's ungentlemanly and personal insults. I, for my part, find it impossible, and as Mr. Herbert, as the Art Society's representative in the question, has broken his engagement with me I find that I am not bound to stand his treatment and refuse to work with him.

"If Mr. Herbert has personal reasons to insult me, his position as conductor of the orchestra does not entitle him to do so during rehearsals and concerts."

The Pittsburgh newspapers featured the complaint under the headline: SAYS HERBERT IS VULGAR.

The members of the orchestra came forward to declare themselves indignant over Borch's action and because of their defense, the Art Society took no notice of the letter. To this day, however, Herbert's men readily recollect the flavor of his tongue-lashings. The lady harpist of the orchestra was frequently a welcome protection.

They also recollect his genuine friendship for them. On one occasion the management decided to reduce the hotel and board money allotted to the orchestra on its spring tour. As the salaries of the leading players were only about fifty dollars a week, Herbert secretly advised them to strike. A letter was drawn up by a committee, demanding no less than two dollars

a day on which to eat and sleep. Herbert approved
it. With his help, the men won.

At another time, the orchestra had an engagement in
Youngstown, Ohio. There was a convention in town
and all accommodations were taken. As the conductor,
a room was found for Herbert, but when he saw a
group of his men sleeping in chairs in the lobby he
took them all into his room. They divided the beds
and floor and table, and Herbert took his few feet of
space with the rest.

"On one of these spring tours," Burck relates, "an
incident happened that pleased him more than any
success with the orchestra. We were waiting in the
Columbus (Ohio) railroad depot. This station has one
of the regular high domes and as Herbert, some of the
other men and myself stood around, he heard the station
man call off the towns at which the departing train
would stop, in the usual sing-song style. The man's
voice rolled all around the station and caught Herbert's
attention. He whispered to us: 'Capucine!'

"This was the word which served us as a text for a
mock chorale which we would sing as an accompaniment to beer. He ranged us around him and suddenly
the station was startled by a male chorus caroling,
'Capucine,' in a severe, religious chant, swelling louder
and louder, with Herbert's baritone above the rest,
until 'Ca-pu-cin-e!' filled the high dome and echoed
back to every corner of the building.

"I have rarely seen a man so pleased as Herbert was

[134]

when we finished. With a broad smile on his lips, he marched us to our train."

The Pittsburgh Orchestra was a favorite in Toronto, where it played at the festivals of the famous Mendelssohn Choir, led by Dr. Voight. Herbert was particularly enthused once over the choir's rendition of a number and when he went on the platform of Massey Hall to congratulate the conductor, he broke into one of his variable dialects—this time Irish.

"That's the best I've heard in voices," he told the audience, "and that's no blarney!"

Andrew Carnegie was an ardent admirer of Victor Herbert. One afternoon, when the orchestra was giving a concert at Carnegie Hall, in New York, Billy Guard, now the publicity director of the Metropolitan Opera House, but then on the staff of the *Morning Telegraph*, saw the steel master strolling in the foyer. Like a good newspaper man he approached him, introduced himself, and inquired how he liked the concert. Carnegie replied:

"My idea of heaven would be to hear Victor Herbert and his men play for me twice every day."

Guard declared himself shocked that Carnegie had not excepted Sunday.

In 1904, after six years' service as conductor, Herbert left the Pittsburgh Orchestra and returned to New York.

HERBERT's association with the Pittsburgh Symphony had in no way interfered with his production of operettas. One of the most popular of all his works, "The Fortune Teller," was composed the year he came to Pittsburgh. The surprising mentality of the man could devote itself every afternoon to rehearsing and studying the interpretation of music of the masters, and in the evening to writing waltzes for ingénues and character songs for comedians.

"The Fortune Teller" was written especially for Alice Nielsen. Frank Perley, the business manager for the Bostonians, organized the Alice Nielsen Opera Company, and Herbert agreed to furnish the music for Miss Nielsen's vehicles. In return for his coöperation he was paid a higher royalty. The singer's explanation of her break with the organization that first sponsored her was given in an interview published in the *Dramatic Mirror*:

"My association with the Bostonians had not been comfortable for some time—not since I made something of a hit in 'The Serenade.' "

Another periodical printed this puckish notice of the separation:

"Miss Nielsen has been for three seasons a leading soprano for Barnabee and MacDonald's company and,

Alice Nielsen in
"The Fortune Teller."

Alice Nielsen in a Scene from "The Singing Girl"

Emma Trentini and Orville Harrold in a Scene
from "Naughty Marietta."

on leaving it a month or so ago, her parting shot was a hint at the old age of almost all the principals with whom she had been associated. Now, if there is one subject more than another upon which the Bostonians are sensitive it is the length of their lives. If you congratulate Mr. Barnabee upon his sprightly walk or Mr. MacDonald upon his rosy cheeks or Mr. Frothingham upon his keen glance, you will stand a very good chance of receiving an order for a box from which to see 'Robin Hood.' The Bostonians, you may be sure, will be the first to read the reviews of the first night of the Nielsen company, and if the articles are not lavishly eulogistic they will be resigned to it."

It probably was differences between Miss Nielsen and Jessie Bartlett Davis—who now had to share her stardom in the company—together with Miss Nielsen's and Perley's ambitions and MacDonald's lingering resentment against the singer, dating from the time Herbert forced him to give her a leading part in "The Serenade," that caused the disruption.

"The Fortune Teller" inveigled another popular member of the Bostonians, Eugene Cowles, to whose good fortune fell the singing of what was to become one of the most popular of all Herbert's songs— "Gypsy Love Song."

The première took place at Wallack's Theatre, on September 26, 1898, with a cast that included Joseph Cawthorne and Marguerita Sylva. The latter, like Miss Nielsen, was later to be well known in grand opera—she was one of the celebrated Carmens—but at that time she was just a lively musical comedy singer who was fond of showing her good legs in black tights. One night during the run of "The Fortune Teller," Miss Nielsen held a little supper party in her hotel, and on a sudden impulse, and in impish mood, she said to Miss Sylva: "Your name isn't Marguerita Sylva at all. I'll bet it's plain Maggie Smith."

Miss Sylva dropped her fork and stared at Miss Nielsen.

"So it is!" she said in a voice small with awe and surprise.

The audiences took to "The Fortune Teller" with fervor from the start. After the second finale—in which a band played on the stage and Miss Nielsen was dazzling in a red hussar uniform—there were many recalls and demands for Herbert and Harry B. Smith, who was again the librettist. Herbert was in the audience and obligingly bowed, but Smith was nowhere to be found. He was known as an inveterate first-night speechmaker, and the disappointed audience yelled for a speech from the prima donna.

"I can't make a speech," she said. "And if I tried, you'd know that."

Some one shouted: "Get Herbert to conduct the march!"

"Come along, Victor!" cried Miss Nielsen, and Victor jumped up, climbed into the pit and beamingly led the orchestra in the requested number.

Incidentally, Smith's speech-making was the cause of the only bad reviews "The Fortune Teller" got.

"I always used to make curtain speeches," he explained, "and for each of the first twenty or thirty pieces I wrote I had a carefully prepared speech in which I took great pride. On the first night of 'The Highwayman,' in New York, I made a speech, saying, among other things, that however much a play might be tried on the road there was only one real first night, and that was in New York.

"It happened that we had played a preliminary engagement in Philadelphia. The papers of the Quaker City took up the matter and construed it as an insult. I received letters saying: 'Wait—wait till you come here with another opera! We will show you where the first nights are!'

"The next production I had in Philadelphia was 'The Fortune Teller,' and the critics roasted it unmercifully. This, however, did not prevent it from being the biggest musical success of that year."

During rehearsals of "The Fortune Teller," an incident happened that illustrates Herbert's extraordinary musical facility. One of the scenes required such a quick change for Miss Nielsen that before she was ready, her cue had been played by the orchestra. In confusion she hopped out on the stage with one boot pulled on and the other in her hand. Herbert stopped the orchestra and, on the minute, wrote into the score ten bars of new music for the tenor, to allow Miss Nielsen more time for her change.

One of the theatre's historic jokes was created in "The Fortune Teller." During a rehearsal, William

Rochester, the stage director, approached Cawthorne with what he decided was a brilliant bit of humor. He was so overcome with the wit of the jest that he had to choke back his laughter when he told it.

"It'll make 'em scream when you include it in the show," he said, and then revealed the masterpiece:

"I had a little bird and its name was Enza.
I opened the cage and in-flu-Enza."

Instead of doubling up, Cawthorne considered.

"It doesn't seem right, Bill," he said at last. "If you opened the cage, *out* flew Enza."

Rochester was unwilling to accept this logic and called over another comedian of the company, Joseph Herbert, to render an opinion. Herbert agreed with Cawthorne.

But Rochester refused to be discouraged and persuaded Cawthorne to try out the joke on the first-night audience. His judgment was entirely vindicated. The ambiguous flight of the little bird, Enza, was greeted with uproarious laughter.

Nevertheless, the joke was always regarded with some doubt by those who had to assume the responsibility of perpetrating it, and when "The Fortune Teller" was revived in 1929 by the Shuberts, Milton Aborn, the director, decided to use his better wisdom and announced: "We'll have to cut that out. The audience will walk out on us."

It was cut out on the opening night, but so strong was Enza's influence that after some reflection, Aborn changed his mind and allowed it in for the second performance. It was received with the same mirthful appreciation that the 1898 audiences gave it.

The following year Herbert did a third piece for Daniels and one for another comedian, Francis Wilson. The Daniels' musical comedy was called, "The Ameer." Of it one New York newspaper critic observed, in a supposed dialogue with a friend:

"There is one man here to-night who enjoyed himself anyhow."

"Who is that?"

"Mr. Daniels."

Another writer went to this extent:

"The names of two grown men (I think it ought to be 'groan' men) appeared on the program at Wallack's Theatre last night as the authors of 'The Ameer,' an opera constructed for Frank Daniels. This was a fortunate interposition of the printer, for the reason that it prevented the audience from falling into the erroneous supposition that the libretto and lyrics had been written by the inmates of a kindergarten for private exhibition purposes. . . . The libretto, which is credited to Kirke La Shelle and Frederick Rancken, is a trivial and infantile affair, without wit or point or grace or anything else that is of the slightest moment."

And later in the long critique, the writer hints at a spat between Smith and Herbert:

"It is to be sincerely hoped that Mr. Herbert will make up his quarrel with Harry B. Smith, who writes lyrics to inspire great musicians. It is a pity if such a musician were to fall permanently into the hands of such literary sausage makers as the ones with whom he is associated in this instance."

"The Ameer" contains nothing memorable in the way of music, and Herbert does not even mind having a brigand "hush" song, with all its painful traditions, including the staccato notes and the marking, *Allegro mysterioso, pp.*

In the same year Herbert and Smith accommodated another comedian with an opera—musical productions with aspiring finales were called operas in those days by their elated composers—and scored another failure. The comedian was Francis Wilson, who took it into his head that Rostand's "Cyrano de Bergerac" should be burlesqued.

Though Herbert's music was an improvement on "The Ameer," "Cyrano" did not quite come off. But three weeks later, yet another Herbert work opened on Broadway, "The Singing Girl," and this was a success.

No less than three operettas in one year! A typical example of Herbert's amazing musical constitution.

Since Herbert always wrote his stage pieces to order, he had a fair knowledge of what would happen to his music when produced. Thus it seems that he only did his best when he was sure of a good singer. There were three first class prima donnas in Herbert's career: Alice Nielsen, Fritzi Scheff and Emma Trentini. They were all familiar to grand opera and it was for them that he wrote his five best-known works: "The Serenade," "The Fortune Teller," "The Singing Girl," "Mlle. Modiste," and "Naughty Marietta."

The libretto of "The Singing Girl"" was written by Stanislaus Stange and only the lyrics by Harry B. Smith. It opened under Perley's management at the Casino Theatre on October 23, 1899, and Alice Nielsen and the tuneful score brought the kind of applause that means success. Rupert Hughes, who was then more inclined to music than to literature, wrote this review of it in *The Criterion:*

"The most fetching thing this town has seen since Cissy Fitzgerald's wink brought a new sensation to a worn old heart, is the mischievous eyelid Alice Nielsen interpolates into her song, 'Beware,' in her new opera, 'The Singing Girl.' And she sings it in the most stunning suit of white silk and silvered doublet ever worn by a girlish boy. And the song itself is one that the whole country will be infected with soon—a lyric as graceful artistically as it is popular.

"When you have said that the company is so fine that it reaches the standard of stock company, that the music of Victor Herbert is at his best and that the costumes are gorgeous, you have said all that you can say. And remembering all these things you will feel a genuine regret that the enterprise seems a certain failure unless the libretto is—not patched-up—but remade. . . . The music by Mr. Herbert dignifies the American stage. It reaches the highest level of European comic opera, particularly in the very elaborate entrance song for

Miss Nielsen. Then, too, it is learnedly humorous. He sprinkles his scores with Attic salt."

Alan Dale provided the salt in the criticism of "The Singing Girl" by adding this paragraph:

"The comedy of the evening was supplied by Mrs. Bartlett Davis (the favorite of the Bostonians) who sat in a box. This lady, by her gestures, her smiles, her ostentatious (ahem!) applause and her almost swooning enthusiasm attracted much attention. Of course I know she didn't intend to do so, but she did it. Her extreme love for Miss Nielsen and her beautiful, almost maternal solicitude for Mr. Cowles (also in the cast) were admirably and scintillantly shown."

In the published score of this operetta there is an elaborate number for "Greta," the main character, called "The Song of the Danube," which was not used in the production after the first few performances. It is really what is known in opera as a "scena," giving a fine opportunity for both the composer and the soprano to distinguish themselves by running through several brands of emotions.

Alice Nielsen did well with it, but by the time the end was reached the watchful Perley noticed that the audience had not produced the volume of handclaps necessary for the usual Nielsen collection of bows and encores. He suggested a substitution. Herbert declined and rushed to the singer.

"You must not let him throw the Danube out!" he said, agitatedly. "You and I have got to stick together on this." Alice promised to stick.

But Perley was insistent.

"Let's try something else just once," he pleaded.

One Sunday afternoon after the first week, Krehbiel dropped in at the Gilsey House to see Miss Nielsen.

"Don't disturb the score," he said. "You must consider your future. Any one can do *those* things, but only an artiste can sing a piece like the Danube."

"I don't know what to do," Alice replied. "I know Victor is heartbroken."

But heartbroken or not, Victor wrote a "Dutch cakewalk" which was substituted at the Monday performance for "The Song of the Danube." He had hopes the audience would dismiss it coldly, but instead, it was accorded eight recalls. The cakewalk was left in, but he would never permit it to be published in the score.

The Alice Nielsen Opera Company was later taken to London where they appeared in the Herbert operettas in the Shaftesbury Theatre, but the venture was not a success. After the return of the company to America, Alice Nielsen remained in Europe, becoming well-known in grand opera. She later achieved her best success in serious music as a concert singer in the United States.

CHAPTER XII

HERBERT's next popular work was "Babes in Toyland," produced in 1903. It was billed as a stupendous extravaganza, but it is remembered to-day principally for the brilliant and pretty "March of the Toys," one of the most frequently played orchestral pieces on the radio to-day. Both on the air and on the stage the melody is used for numerous purposes and is one of those which familiarity does not stale to an appreciable degree.

Glen MacDonough, who wrote the book and lyrics, had a clever song in it called, "I Can't Do That Sum," which became a favorite and helped spread the fame of the musical comedy. Here is the first verse and the chorus:

"If a steamship weighed ten thousand tons,
And sailed five thousand miles,
With a cargo large of overshoes,
And carving knives and files;
If the mates were almost six feet high,
And the bos'n near the same—
Would you subtract or multiply,
To find the captain's name?

CHILDREN'S CHORUS

"Oh!—
Put down six and carry two,
Gee, but this is hard to do!

You can think and think and think,
Till your brains are numb;
I don't care what teacher says,
I can't do that sum."

In the same year, Herbert wrote "Babette," and
while that is a forgotten item of the Herbert repertory,
it is important because it was written for Fritzi Scheff,
and was followed by "Mlle. Modiste," an operetta with
which her name is permanently coupled.

Fritzi Scheff came to Herbert by way of the Metropolitan Opera House. She was the daughter of a leading soprano at the Frankfort Opera House and was
born in Vienna. The combination made her a vivacious,
temperamental person, who, from her first appearance
in New York opera, became a talk of the town.

During a rehearsal of Paderewski's seldom-played
opera, "Manru," at the Metropolitan, the composer
became very irritable, even desperate, as everything
seemed to go wrong. Fritzi, taking pity on his strained
nerves, seized a tambourine and swept into a dance.

The relieving interlude brought laughter from singers and orchestra. Paderewski merely glared at her.
He threw his sensitive fingers into his beautiful and
celebrated hair, as if this were the last straw. But the
impregnable Viennese was undisturbed, and her giddy
dance increased rather than abated. In a few moments
the helpless pianist broke into a laugh, too.

"What a little devil you are!" he exclaimed.

This incident was diligently broadcast, and from then

on the delighted newspapers faithfully referred to Fritzi as "the little devil of the Metropolitan."

Fritzi sang principal rôles in opera, but her natural opera comique temperament made the life of a routine diva difficult for her. Apart from that, she exhibited a straightforward temperament which added to the gayeties of an operatic back-stage.

Whenever a personality of her type appears in American grand opera theatrical managers immediately become attentive. Charles Dillingham saw in Fritzi a potential musical comedy star. Knowing he could wean her from grand opera only by a high salary, he interested Charles Frohman, with whom he was friendly, to back him. Frohman agreed, and Dillingham began to make overtures, based on a melody of a thousand dollars a week.

This was during Fritzi's third season at the Metropolitan. Others had tried to induce Fraulein Scheff to appear on Broadway proper, but negotiations had fallen through. She was more interested in Dillingham's proposals. Then an incident occurred which may have been the deciding influence that gave Victor Herbert another Alice Nielsen.

In the spring of 1903, the Metropolitan Company was touring. Mozart's "Magic Flute" was performed, with Sembrich as the "Queen of the Night" and Fritzi as "Papagena." It was a good part for Miss Scheff, and after a duet with "Papageno," sung by Campanari, there was much applause, sprinkled with shouts of: "Scheff!"

Several times the singers were recalled and Fritzi gratefully kissed her finger-tips, and shook her head to indicate she would take no more calls. Mme. Sembrich now came out to sing her final aria, but as the applause did not subside, the eminent artiste turned her back on the audience and walked off the stage.

The opera was finished without Mme. Sembrich, and when calls came for her after the final curtain, Fritzi frankly shouted to the audience: "She has gone home!"

Fritzi appeared no more at the Metropolitan. Dillingham had her signed to a contract, and in the fall of the year she made her comic opera début in "Babette," by Herbert and Smith. It opened at the Broadway Theatre on November 16, 1903.

"Babette" was but a moderate success for the producer, but a decided personal triumph for the prima donna. The audience greeted her numbers enthusiastically, and after the second act, she pulled Herbert on the stage and gave him a warm hug and kiss.

It was a significant kiss. The press agents made a lot of it and the newspapers were obliging. The incident probably impressed itself on Herbert and undoubtedly was responsible for the words set to the closing phrases of the "Kiss Me Again" song in "Mlle. Modiste."

Even though publicity made up a good deal of the "Babette" kiss stories, it is amazing what genuine interest an actress's non-professional kiss of a man in full view of an audience aroused. Every interviewer ques-

tioned Fritzi at length about it until at last she protested in her mixed English:

"I'm dead of that kiss. So much has been said about
it—about one little, tiny kiss. Some said it was what
you call a grand-stand play. That is all nuisance. I did
not know anything about it. I did not know I was going
to kiss Victor Herbert until it was all over. Everybody
was so kind and I was so glad and Mr. Herbert, he say
so many nice things to me."

Two seasons later, Fritzi appeared in the greatest
success of her career, and one of Herbert's most popular, if not *the* most popular, operettas—"Mlle. Modiste." The book and lyrics were written by Mr. Henry
M. Blossom, who was known at that time as the author
of "Checkers."

"Mlle. Modiste" opened at the Knickerbocker Theatre on December 25, 1905, after an out-of-town run,
which included Chicago. In Washington, it was seen
by a presidential party, consisting of President Roose-
velt and his wife, Secretary of State Root, and Justice
and Mrs. Holmes. During the intermission, Herbert
took keen pleasure in stepping into the conductor's
place and leading the orchestra in "The Star-Spangled
Banner." The president rewarded him by joining heartily in the applause.

This operetta contains more catchy tunes than any
other of Herbert's stage works. No less than five are
known on Broadway as being in the "hit" class, and
one, while not so tuneful, is popular because of its

lyric and attendant character comedy: "I Want What I Want When I Want It."

The "hits" are: "Kiss Me Again," "The Mascot of the Troop," "The Time, the Place and the Girl," "Hats Make the Woman," and the charming trio, "When the Cat's Away the Mice Will Play." With the exception of the latter, all these are standard pieces in the literature of light music to-day, and "The Mascot" is familiar as a march. To these melodies may be added the shop-girls' opening chorus, an apt setting to an apt lyric—

"Furs and feathers, buckles, bows!
Some of these—some of those!"

Herbert regarded "Mlle. Modiste" highly, from a musical standpoint, and although it rises easily to the level of good comic opera, it is rather difficult to understand the following comment on its composition which Herbert wrote for the first number of an obscure New York musical magazine called *Tone* (April, 1908):

"I confess that when I wrote 'Mlle. Modiste' it was with a dull dread in my heart that the public would reject it and cast it into ignominious seclusion from which it would never return. On the opening night I felt like a man going to the gallows. I was doubtful that the 'dear public,' which all playwrights fear and at the same time love, was in the right frame of mind to accept a musical production composed of anything but a conglomeration of vaudeville acts and so-called popular songs woven together with an apology of a plot.

"I cannot express the gratification I felt on the following morning when I awoke and found that I had been deceived in my friends, the public; that after all they had welcomed with outstretched hands the musical play that was a little better than the vaudeville musical atrocities heretofore offered.

"It was mainly the encouragement Mr. Blossom and I received in the reception of our little French milliner that spurred us on to write 'The Red Mill.'"

"Mlle. Modiste" is not as high-flown as all that. It is more for the public than "The Serenade," written years back.

The most famous song from "Mlle. Modiste" is, of course, "Kiss Me Again"—which is not its actual title at all. The composition is officially known as, "If I Were On the Stage," and is part of one of Herbert's favorite extended numbers. It really consists of a prologue and three acts. In the beginning, "Fifi," the main character, sings:

> "If I were asked to play the part,
>   Of simple maiden, light of heart,
>   A village lass in country clothes,
>   As to and from her work she goes,
>   I'd sing a merry, lilting strain,
>   And gayly dance to this refrain:"

A gavotte follows, after which an interlude expresses Fifi's desire to play the rôle of an historical French lady. A polonaise is introduced, and then comes:

Fritzi Scheff in "Mlle. Modiste."

Mary Garden in "Louise."

"But best of all the parts I'd play,
If I could only have my way,
Would be a strong romantic rôle,
Emotional and full of soul.
And I believe, for such a thing,
A dreamy, sensuous waltz I'd sing—"

This leads into "Sweet Summer Breeze—"

Though the music that precedes the waltz is two-thirds of the complete composition, it is musically no more than an introduction, a sort of melodious comic opera recitative.

"Kiss me Again" has a romantic story apart from its text. Herbert himself told it to a group of friends who were chatting with him in a Boston hotel:

"I was giving a series of concerts at Saratoga and the orchestra was engrossing my attention. We had some splendid concerts, and our programs were most popular. In the midst of the engagement Henry Blossom came up from New York. He had been writing the libretto of 'Mlle. Modiste,' and he was convinced that an outstanding melody was a real necessity. He hadn't any notion what the lyric should be, but in a way he thought it should be something ingratiating for Miss Scheff to sing.

"We couldn't make any headway. Little melodies came to me, but not one that seemed to be the kind needed. You see, the orchestra and the concerts were uppermost in my mind.

"After a few days, Blossom went back to New York. I was rather perturbed, but still I didn't concentrate.

[153]

At length I decided it was foolish of me not to get somewhere and I put on pressure. That night I had the matter in mind when I went to bed. Suddenly the melody came to me. I rose and turned on the gas. Then I jotted down the thirty-two bars that were my inspiration. I felt I had conquered. Then I went to sleep.

"In the morning when I awoke I thought I could hum the melody. But it had passed out of my mind. I couldn't believe that already I had forgotten music that had been so clear in my mind the night before. I picked up the manuscript. Yes, that was the melody. So I notified Charles Dillingham, Miss Scheff and Henry Blossom. Imagine my surprise when each of them said it was charming, but probably wouldn't do at all. However, Henry set out to write the lyric, and then Miss Scheff was given the ballad to sing.

" 'It is written too low at the beginning,' was the comment.

" 'That was my intention,' I asserted. 'A woman's voice, when low, is always appealing, and the song rises to heights.'

"I could see every one was dubious and I felt rather abashed. Miss Scheff sang the aria again, beautifully; there was no denying that. Yet still there seemed to be doubt. I changed the key, but otherwise the melody remained as originally written.

"Then, at last, I got some encouragement. John Lunt, of Buffalo, heard the song and he was entranced.

" 'It is beautiful,' he said. That settled it."

Between the writing of "Mlle. Modiste" and "Naughty Marietta," which was produced in 1910, and ranks as the best of all his light operas, Herbert wrote many works, but only two were outstanding successes —"The Red Mill," and "It Happened in Nordland." The former was produced in 1905, and the latter in 1906.

As almost every one who has any interest in the theater knows, "The Red Mill" was the great starring vehicle of Montgomery and Stone. It was probably their biggest hit, and is memorable among famous Broadway profit-makers. And yet, before it opened, Charles Dillingham was ready to sell out and wash his hands of it, so convinced was he that it would be a flat failure.

At the last rehearsals, when everything should have assumed the high polish of a successful production, it became increasingly evident to Dillingham and some others connected with the piece that they were in for trouble. This was particularly distressing to the producer since Montgomery and Stone had broken their contract with the estate of Frank Hamlin, who had produced their last great success, "The Wizard of Oz," to appear in the Herbert and Blossom operetta.

The cast assembled for the final rehearsal on Saturday at the Knickerbocker Theatre in New York, where "The Red Mill" was to open. They worked steadily until four-thirty on Sunday morning. Every one's nerves were frayed, every one was dead tired, and all the principals were downhearted. All the principals, that is, but one—Victor Herbert.

His nerves were unruffled; he was not tired. Instead, he was irritatingly cheerful and optimistic. All those long hours he had stood in the orchestra pit, rehearsing patiently, and giving all help that was needed. His vitality seemed inexhaustible, and had it not been that so depressing a spirit hung over the empty hollowness of the dark theatre, the company would have admired him as a superman.

At last the weary rehearsing came to an end. The company dispersed. Herbert, with extraordinary buoyancy, gathered together Dillingham, Fred Stone, Dave Montgomery, Fred Latham, the director, and Henry Blossom, the librettist, and led them into the basement bar of the Normandy Hotel (gone to-day, as is the Knickerbocker Theatre) for breakfast.

After the regulation bacon, scrambled eggs and coffee—which cheered the downcast group but little—Herbert ordered champagne and a bottle of Worcestershire sauce. As the others looked on wonderingly, he took each wine glass, tilted it, and poured in a few drops of the sauce. Then he rolled the glass carefully until the condiment covered half its circumference with a thin, dark smudge.

Into these glasses Herbert poured the champagne, explaining that the combination was a wonderful tonic for depressed spirits. Whether it was the champagne or the Worcestershire, the drink did invigorate them all. But what remained as an imperishable souvenir of that dark dawn at the Normandy was the fantastic champagne cocktail.

After the pre-production fog had been lifted by enthusiastic audiences, "The Red Mill" became notable, also, for introducing the first moving sign on Broadway. Harry Somers, the manager of the Knickerbocker, was struck with the idea of emulating Coney Island by putting up on the wall of the theatre the four wings of a windmill, illumined by red lamps. He outlined his plan to the stage electrician, Jim Pennyfeather, who suggested an improvement by installing a little motor in the sign to make the wings turn.

Somers went to Alf Hayman, his superior in the theatre, with the joint idea.

"How much will it cost?" Hayman asked.

"Oh, a couple of hundred dollars," Somers guessed.

Hayman gave his consent and thus made Broadway lighting history. Later, of course, the motor in electric signs was used, not to operate moving objects, but to manipulate the complex system of switches which control thousands of flashing bulbs in an illusion of moving.

A picture of Victor Herbert and of his standing on Broadway at this time was given by the late Charles K. Harris in his autobiography, "After the Ball." Harris, after establishing himself as a successful song-writer and publisher, was anxious to extend his business.

"My ambition," he said, "was to sign up Victor Herbert for just one show. His name on my catalog would mean a great deal to me.

[157]

" 'Just have a little patience, C. K.,' Joe Weber told me. 'You never can tell what will happen.'

"When his second show was about to close, Joe sent for me.

" 'Charlie,' he said, 'my next show is going to be of a higher order than we have been doing lately. The dialogue and lyrics will be written by Edgar Smith and the music by Victor Herbert. It is going to be called 'Dream City and the Magic Knight.'

"I stood looking at him and gasped. 'You don't mean to say, Joe, that Victor Herbert is going to write the music?'

" 'Sure,' said he. 'Why not?'

" 'But where do I get off?'

" 'You are to publish the music.'

"But I understand he is under contract with another publisher, and has been, for several years. In fact, he is a silent partner in the concern.'

" 'That's makes no difference to me, C. K.; you publish the music. So that settles that.' And so it did.

"That was my first meeting with the celebrated composer, Victor Herbert. What a pleasure it was to work with such an artist! His scores were sent to my office intact. All he wished to see were the printers' proofs. No other arranger or musician touched his manuscripts and everything went like clockwork. I spread myself on the title page as well as over the vocal score. Herbert was thoroughly surprised when the opening night came and the music, as well as the score, was ready for the market. I shall never forget the pleased look on his face when I handed him the first vocal score of 'Dream City and the Magic Knight.' He must have been pleased with my work as well as with my royalty statements, for he sent me his next score to publish. This was 'Algeria,' which many musicians consider one of his best scores. I later also published 'Little Nemo,' book by Harry M. Smith, and score by Victor Herbert."

Some years later Herbert was not as scrupulous about his scores as Harris indicates. He employed a musical secretary, Harold Sanford, to whom he turned over sketches for the orchestration of the operettas. Sanford was so familiar with the composer's style that he was able to complete the scores from Herbert's musical shorthand markings.

Another interesting reminiscence of Herbert in that period is given in a letter written by Harry C. Freeborn, of Philadelphia, a writer whose interest in libretto composition led him to an acquaintance with the composer. Among other things, Mr. Freeborn wrote:

"At rehearsals Victor was very exacting, his criticisms were sometimes caustic, and spiced with a genial profanity which, however, left no rancor. He would stand in the pit, with a sleeveless green vest, without collar or tie, with the perspiration streaming down his face, even in mid-winter. Indeed, I never saw any one perspire quite so profusely as he. He would address each man in his native tongue, frequently changing from English to German to French to Italian, all in a few minutes. But when the nervous tension became strained, and he saw that the men were growing restive under the lash, he would stop the proceedings, and tell a funny story. Instantly good humor was restored.

"He at one time sought to test his popularity and wrote 'Al Fresco' under the name of 'Frank Roland.' It became popular at once and afterwards he incorporated it in 'It Happened in Nordland.'

"On the matter of his lack of skill in his selection of librettos much has been written since his death, but he told me he often had three hundred librettos sent him in a year, but had never yet found one suited to his requirements in all the multitudes that came unsolicited. This was because the aspirants had not the technique of the trade.

"Herbert possessed a memory that to me seemed colossal, and I do not mean in a musical sense. His recollection of facts and events was photographic in its accuracy. He was also intensely sentimental. One day at Willow Grove Park (where Herbert gave summer orchestral concerts for many years) the superintendent announced his intention of cutting down a shabby Norway spruce which grew outside the window of Herbert's study. He pleaded with the man not to do this, because 'It was a little fellow only four feet high when I came to the park fifteen years ago, and I have watched it grow, year by year.'

"Always he was eager to aid the amateur composer in search of constructive criticism. In addition to his musical facets he was a brilliant and witty talker. His delivery was animated, vivacious and punctuated with humorous observations and always highly entertaining."

It was in May, 1904, that Herbert published "Al Fresco," under the assumed name of "Frank Roland." But as a test of the influence his reputation carried, this composition was a poor choice. "Al Fresco" is among a select group of Herbert's best melodies, and is likely to survive as a semi-classic. It would have become popular no matter whose name was attached to it. If anything, this incident proves that a good melody needs no reputation for its composer to bring it success.

"Al Fresco" was originally written as an intermezzo for the piano. In "It Happened in Nordland," it is used in the opening chorus of the second act. The coquettish first part is played by the orchestra, with the chorus singing an obligato. The slower movement that follows is given to the voices.

The lyric which Glen MacDonough set to this music is a fine example of the skill which Herbert is said to have found lacking in the three hundred librettos he received in a year. This is it:

> "Sweet love to-day our queen is,
> Now o'er each lightly beating heart,
> She holds full sway!
> Joy everywhere supreme is!
> For while sweet love and folly reign,
> We'll scoff at care!"

Note the charming effect of "queen is," and "supreme is," which is heightened by coming, as it does, at the end of a phrase, and by "is" falling an interval of a third down the scale.

Herbert did receive many librettos, but his rejection

of them had little to do with their merit. Libretto writing has always been an inside business, and outsiders cannot break in unless great personal effort is added to the efficiency of the librettist's work.

XIII

A reminiscence of Victor Herbert, dating from this prime of his life, and presenting him in the lively light in which Broadway professionals knew him, was written by Theodore Stearns for the *New York Morning Telegraph*. It follows:

"I first met Victor Herbert in the days when the old Aschenbroedel clubhouse, up in East Eighty-sixth Street, was the holy of holies for the post-graduate musicians of New York City. Herbert was rehearsing his orchestra there for the coming summer concert season in Willow Grove Park, Philadelphia. He had accepted an Indian Suite of mine for orchestra, and Bob Iverson, his manager, had phoned me that the composition was to be rehearsed that day and that Herbert wanted me to be there.

"As I entered the rehearsal room the 'old man,' as we affectionately called him, looked around, laid down his baton and walked briskly over to the door.

" 'You Mr. Stearns?' he inquired. I nodded, too happy to speak. 'All right, my boy,' he said, genially. 'Your suite sounds good. A little academic, but what the hell? Damn' horn players! If one note is copied wrong in their parts, they always stand up and say the whole thing is a piece of cheese.'

"A few weeks later Ned Wayburn said to me: 'Do you know Victor Herbert?'

" 'Yes.'

" 'Lew Fields needs a music director for Herbert's "The Rose of Algeria" but it's up to Herbert himself. Can you get to him?' But I was already out of the door and on the way to Philadelphia.

"Three hours later, in Willow Grove Park, I walked up to the bandroom during the intermission of the concert. The old man came puffing in and started tearing off his collar and shirt. He always changed them between the acts.

" 'Hello, my boy!' he shouted cordially. 'Damn this collar button! Did you ever see such heat? Your Indian Suite went all right. What brings you here?'

"I made known my mission and Herbert was all business at once.

" 'Well, I know you as a composer,' he said thoughtfully. 'I know that you are a good musician but I never saw you conduct.' At this point Bob Iverson told him something and Herbert made one of his lightning decisions. 'I'd better play some of the "Algeria" music during the next half of the concert—damn this collar button!' Turning to me he said: 'I'm not kidding myself that I'm a Richard Wagner, but any ass can see that my music has to be conducted carefully and you've never heard it. I'll play the "Rose of Algeria" selections and you listen, my boy.'

"That night Herbert, Johnny Spargur, his concert master, Iverson and myself talked about everything

[164]

under the sun, including music and the intrinsic worth of Wurzburger beer.

"We opened in Wilkes-Barre with 'The Rose of Algeria' to calm ruffled temperaments and smooth off the rough edges. During the rehearsal the preceding night one of the chorus men dropped out.

" 'What's the matter with him?' asked Herbert, who was in a side aisle with a pilot light, writing some 'hurry music.'

" 'He's hungry,' I answered. I had heard the dressing-room talk.

"In a second Herbert was on the stage. He shoved a twenty-dollar bill into the fellow's hand and clapped him on the back.

" 'Go out and eat your head off,' said Vic. 'Have a drink on me, too—five or six of them, if you like— what the hell!'

"Did that chorus sing? I'll say they did. Herbert ever afterwards was their god.

"In those days, Herbert invariably conducted the opening performances of his light operas, but he wouldn't do it in Wilkes-Barre. Arriving in Philadelphia, where the show really opened, he told me I must sit in the orchestra pit right next to him. The reason for this was that Herbert seldom knew the music cues. Before we went into the pit, he cautioned me to give him a punch just before the cues came.

" 'If I conduct too fast,' he said, 'just pull my coat-tail. If I'm going too slow, jab me in the leg.'

"He was a scream when he played his scores on the

piano for a musical director. After we took a drink, he would sit down on the piano stool, rap the keyboard once or twice with the back of his hand, and keep up a running fire of stories, explanations and reminiscences. Descending the bass passages, he usually finished up with a grunt, and if he missed fire technically now and then, he'd damn pianos in general.

"During a rehearsal of 'The Rose of Algeria,' a dancer wanted Herbert to alter the tempo of the music, claiming it was too fast for him.

" 'What's that?' roared Herbert, striding down the aisle. 'My music is as good as your dance. You change your feet instead of wanting me to change my tempos. While we're about it,' he added, pointing to our soubrette, 'you stop holding that high note in my song as long as you do. Where do you think you are? In Italy?'

"After that there was never any trouble with the musical director."

There is yet another glimpse of Herbert at this time from the recollections of William Raymond Sill, printed in the *New York Review:*

"Before we ever knew Victor Herbert personally we recall him as the greatest cello player that ever came to America. . . . And this being so we feel constrained to recall an incident that happened in Wilkes-Barre, Pennsylvania, the other night, on the occasion of a dress rehearsal of 'The Rose of Algeria.'

"Mr. Fields and Mr. Herbert were sitting in the body of the house. The orchestra was playing 'Ask

Her While the Band Is Playing.' The lyric of this song calls for much instrumentation, the words being:

'Ask her while the band is playing,
  Let the cornet speak for you;
While the cello, soft and mellow,
  Aids the winsome maid to woo."

" 'Excuse me, Lew,' said Mr. Herbert suddenly and leapt up from his seat. Vaulting over the brass rail of the orchestra pit, he took the bow from the cello player and played his own conception of how the cello should be soft and mellow to win the obdurate maid.

"And at this point the voice of a stage hand rang out as clear as that of the tones of the Sultan on Christmas Eve: 'Say, bo, who's that guy buttin' in on this rehearsal with the big fiddle?'

"Everybody but Mr. Herbert himself was amazed; but he only laughed.

"Not long ago we were sent to Mr. Herbert's summer home—Camp Joyland, at Lake Placid—at the behest of Mr. Fields, for, be it known, Mr. Herbert is writing the music for Mr. Fields' personal starring venture, 'Old Dutch.'

"As we drove up in the bus, we saw a stout man playing baseball with a lot of youths of younger growth. He was playing good ball, too, for he had just captured a hot liner and had fielded it to first, scoring a double play. When the game was over and his side had won, he took us into his bungalow. And there, by the hearthstone, was his beloved cello. Instinctively he reached for it, and even as we conversed he drew from it the strains of 'The Low-Backed Car.' There are several million people in this wide world of ours who would have given a lot to have heard that melody as only Herbert can play it, and as only Herbert's cello can sigh and sing."

Mr. Sill's version of the "Ask Her While the Band Is Playing" incident varies from another, which has the stage hand bawling: "Say—who's that fat guy playing the big fiddle?"

A year before "The Rose of Algeria"—an attractive piece but hardly deserving the legend that seems to have grown up on Broadway that it is a Herbert masterpiece—Fritzi Scheff was provided with another operetta by Blossom and Herbert. That was "The Prima Donna." It did not equal "Mlle. Modiste," as was hoped, and after a fair success, slipped out of sight, rarely to be heard of again. "The Prima Donna" was supposed to be founded on certain incidents in Fritzi's life as a temperamental opera singer and Henry Blossom wrote a number of what might be called epigrams to go with the idea. For example:

"To breathe right you've got to believe that you're a two-story building and then you sing from the basement, not from the parlor."

"Prima donnas ought to act for nothing, and draw money for rehearsals."

A few more of the librettist's lines from the same work may be useful in providing a picture of the higher class musical comedy humor of that day:

"If you're lucky in love, you've *got* to be lucky in cards."

"I can tell you, wherever she is, she writes you often."
"How can you tell?"
"You know where to look for the second page."

(This quip, of course, refers to the various methods of organizing a folder of note-paper.)

"All things come to him who waits on himself."

"Oh, my dear baron, I'm sorry to hear that your wife has run away with your chauffeur."
"Yes, and he was such an excellent chauffeur, too."

"Oh, doctor, is it true that people are buried alive?"
"None of my patients are."

Herbert wrote one more operetta for Miss Scheff. It was a failure. It was first titled "The Duchess," but later went under the name of "Mlle. Rosita." The discouraging reception of the piece (produced by Lee and J. J. Shubert) irritated Fritzi so much that her temperamental outbursts held the company in a continual state of suspense as to the future. This condition inspired Jack Hazzard, the comedian of "Mlle. Rosita," to pen the following stanza:

"Now I lay me off again,
    I shall resume, the Lord knows when;
If they should close before I wake,
    Give my regards to Lee and Jake."

Despite her close association with Herbert's music, Miss Scheff, who shortly before the time of this writing made a successful return to the stage, has but a vague remembrance of the composer.

"It is strange," she declares, "that I should be so familiarly connected in the public mind with Victor Herbert, and know so little about him. When I first sang in his operettas my English was too bad to know any Americans intimately. And later we hardly met, socially. When he made an appearance at rehearsals, he relied chiefly upon his conductors, and so we had little to do with one another. Our friendship consisted of a tap on the shoulder by him, with a 'How are you, Fritzi?' and nothing more. I was never even in his home, and never met his wife.

"We used to have some differences over the music. Herbert had a peculiarity of adding codas to his songs. I considered these anticlimaxes and protested. It sometimes came to the point where I would refuse to sing the song, and he refuse to change it. But eventually I sang it—his way. I thought that he was too much influenced by the cello in his writing for the voice and told him so. His music often had too low a range for a soprano.

"My most distinct memory of him is his pleasant smile and his sweet manners. Of course, he could be angry. He had his Irish temper and I had my Austrian one. When we clashed there was a little excitement.

" 'Kiss Me Again' was without words when it was first played for me. Mr. Dillingham called me over to his office one day and told me that Herbert had written a waltz song for me. The now famous lyric was added later."

It is of interest to insert in the summary of this period of Herbert's life, a part of an analytical article written by the well-known music critic, Henry T. Parker, in the *Boston Transcript* in 1907. Herbert's old operetta, "The Wizard of the Nile," composed in 1895, and his latest production, "The Tattooed Man," were both being played in Boston. Mr. Parker took advantage of the coincidence to compare the musicianship of the two works:

". . . The comparison is not altogether flattering to Mr. Herbert. True, 'The Tattooed Man' is a musical play, rather than an operetta in the old sense of the word; while the second act (which missed fire in the original performances last spring) has been so altered, padded and generally messed about that it is hard to tell what is and what is not Mr. Herbert's.

"In the years in which Mr. Herbert wrote 'The Wizard of the Nile,' he took pains steadily. Now he takes them only intermittently. He is always in a hurry, always ready for new 'business,' until the pile of commissions on his table must be almost as high as the piles of manuscript that is to discharge them. In 'Mlle. Modiste' as Fritzi Scheff sang it for two years, it was easy to discover when Mr. Herbert was taking pains and when he was turning off his music in the easiest way. The painstaking 'numbers' often had the best music and the air of gay spontaneity that he flung over them hid his care.

"In the rest he plied unhesitatingly the advantages that he has long had over most American composers of his kind and that have been his refuge when he was hurried, tired or sterile. Time and again the average writer of the songs in current musical plays can only pick out on the piano the tune that has come into his head. Sometimes he cannot even put it to paper in musical notation. He can no more develop it musically or score it for a small orchestra than he could with a symphony. Strings, winds, and brass, with all the color and contrast, the dramatic pith and comic point that they give in musical plays, are a sealed book to him. Some poor and nameless devil, who can turn his musical knowledge to no other uses, takes down the song writer's tune, gives it sufficient length, and puts some sort of an instrumental 'hand-me-down' upon it. If the melody in itself happens to catch the popular ear, 'it goes,' and the song has fulfilled its purpose.

"Mr. Herbert, on the other hand, is an accomplished musician. He can develop a melody into something more than repetition; he is not confined to elementary rhythms and modulations; he can build solidly an opening chorus or a final ensemble; he knows how to call each group of instruments in his orchestra to his aid and to the pleasure of his audience. No one is better aware of these advantages than Mr. Herbert himself. He used them in his hurried or lazy moments in 'Mlle. Modiste' and he uses them from beginning to end of his music in 'The Tattooed Man'. . . . Some of the despised song-smiths have invented quite as good tunes for musical plays as most that Mr. Herbert has put into 'The Tattooed Man.' Yet while the audience listens he persuades it to believe that they are very good tunes indeed. He makes the orchestra give color and atmosphere to his opening chorus and his listeners like it. . . . The more serious numbers in 'The Wizard of the Nile' have melodies that please or charm independently of the instrument and rhythmic ornaments. . . .

"It has been only fair to rank Mr. Herbert with the ablest writers of similar music in Europe. At his best, indeed, he excels many of them. Unfortunately that best lies more and more in his earlier work—before he was a composer in a hurry."

Herbert did rely upon his skill with the orchestra and chorus to cover up deficiencies. He had an almost fatalistic belief that any melody he wrote would "come out well," after he orchestrated it. He had a similar faith that, no matter what silly plot or commonplace solo numbers an operetta contained, his ensembles, and especially his finales, would lift it to success.

Those Herbert "finales" were famous on Broadway. In his later years, when he fell out of step with the tendencies of modern musical productions and his successes were few, much of his work consisted of writing finales for revues.

All his operettas are based on an unvarying formula. Each act has an elaborate opening chorus, a few solo numbers, and an elaborate finale. About half of each work is taken up by these concerted pieces. Often the result is monotony and lack of imaginativeness. It is true, of course, that comic operas are generally built on this plan, but given a large stock of productions by one man, all plotted along the same lines and all carrying the same spirit, the conventionality is accentuated. Yet to Herbert, these inevitable ensembles were necessary. They were shelters to which he could run when inspiration failed, or when there was not time enough for other work, or when there was not the desire to wait for inspiration.

In May, 1907, Herbert and George V. Hobart put into vaudeville a skit they had formerly written for a Lambs Club entertainment, called "The Song Birds." It was a satire on the operatic warfare being waged then between Heinrich Conried, the Metropolitan Opera House director and Oscar Hammerstein, rival impresario of the Manhattan Opera House. It contained a scene which since has been often duplicated in vaudeville and revues. Oscar's singers and Conried's singers were drawn up on opposite sides of the stage in full battle array, and each tried to sing the other down. This idea later was transformed into the familiar contest between classical music and jazz.

In 1910, Herbert wrote the best operetta of his career—"Naughty Marietta." It was produced at the New York Theatre on November 7, and under somewhat romantic circumstances.

The New York Theatre was the most magnificent theatrical gesture the great Oscar Hammerstein made. He built it at a time when Times Square was a ramshackle neighborhood by day and a forlorn and deserted one by night. It was called "the deadline."

Oscar had been part owner of the Koster and Bial

Music Hall, at Broadway and Thirty-fourth Street, and had been bought out after he had hissed one of his own performers.

A fight had followed, and Oscar spent some time in jail. The break came when his partners refused to bail him out. With the money he received for his share of the enterprise, he declared he would ruin his late associates. He thereupon built an immense three-sectional theater on Broadway, between Forty-fourth and Forty-fifth Streets, and called it the Olympia. It housed a musical hall, a theater, a concert hall and some other things.

Koster and Bial's Music Hall did close—but so did the Olympia. It was an enterprise before its time. The New York Insurance Company foreclosed on a mortgage of almost a million dollars, and Oscar was heartbroken. He refused to leave the theater, and had to be torn away from his barricades. Then he vowed that as long as he lived he would never set foot in the building, or walk on that side of the street.

Time went by and Oscar became an operatic impresario with the determination of crushing the Metropolitan Opera House through his superior performances at the Manhattan Opera House. He did accomplish great things, introducing new and important operas, and singers like John McCormack and Mary Garden.

But the Metropolitan had the money, and money wore down even the iron stamina of Oscar Hammerstein. He was almost bankrupt when his son Arthur negotiated a deal with the older opera house to buy the Hammerstein operatic properties for over a million dollars. A stipulation, however, provided that Oscar was not to produce grand opera in certain American territories for ten years.

Oscar was in London when this matter went through and he raged to the skies that he had been betrayed. But Arthur had his father's power of attorney. When the older Hammerstein came back to New York—after having made arrangements to lose all his new funds in an opera house in London which was to rival Covent Garden—he decided to use some of his song birds in comic opera, since he could not produce grand opera.

"Naughty Marietta" was one of the Hammerstein productions-of-necessity, and Emma Trentini and Orville Harold, both of the Manhattan Opera House, sang the principal rôles.

Emma Trentini was a little Italian girl with a marvelous throat and a vivacious spirit. She was known —like Fritzi Scheff—as the "little devil" of her own opera house, and comic opera suited her, too, better than the more serious brand. Harold, of course, had already established a reputation as a fine tenor and a good actor.

With such singers, and with Hammerstein as the producer, Herbert could satisfy himself in all that he wanted to do in comic opera.

To give still more interest to the proceedings, "Naughty Marietta" was to open at the old Olympia Theatre, renamed the New York Theatre, which Oscar had left with such bitterness twelve years before. He had to break his vow to be at the première of his own production, but he broke it, and as a reward, the press of New York gave him columns of publicity. His reëntrance into the theater was effected in this way:

On Sunday evening before the opening night, when all the members of the cast had reported for the dress rehearsal, Arthur Hammerstein gave the stage-door man a dollar and told him to get a beer and stay away for a little while. Then he locked the door and returned to the stage. He called to Herbert, who was waiting in the pit to begin rehearsing, to wait a few minutes.

At half-past eight, there was a knock at the door. Arthur waited, and the company became silent and expectant. The door rattled violently, and then again. Arthur threw it open and said, laughingly: "All right, dad, come in!"

The famous top-hatted and cigared personality strode in. Ben Teal, the stage manager, and Herbert rushed forward to shake his hand. The entire company gave a series of rousing cheers. Hammerstein held up his hand.

"Wait till I get a good look at it!"

He walked to the edge of the stage, Arthur following him, and looked into the dark interior. He stood there for five minutes, silent and motionless. Then he turned to his company.

"All right, ladies and gentlemen. Go ahead with your play. You see, I felt exactly as you do. I needed a rehearsal for to-morrow."

"Naughty Marietta," written around a romantic creole plot, was a success for all concerned—with the usual reservations about the libretto, written by Rida Johnson Young. It takes its place beside "Robin Hood," "The Serenade," "The Fortune Teller" and "Mlle. Modiste." They are the five best comic operas created in America. And it is the last word in tribute to Victor Herbert to point out that he wrote four of them.

A review of the première in *Musical America* justly describes the music:

". . . Most of Victor Herbert's music ranks among the very best of his career. Keeping in mind the circumstances under which his opera was to be produced, he was scrupulous to eliminate such banal material as he had sometimes been previously compelled to furnish as a concession to Broadway's exactions in the way of 'topical' songs. 'Naughty Marietta' does contain some numbers in which the verses smack of flippancy, but the composer has consistently prevented his music from degenerating into a trivial support for the reciting voice.

"For the rest, to point out the noteworthy pieces would require a mention of almost everything in the score. On the first night every number was encored. The opening is a finely-wrought tone-picture of the dawning day. This is followed in rapid succession by a sprightly ensemble, 'Taisez-Vous,' and by a charming little air, 'Naughty Marietta,' for the heroine. 'If I Were Anybody Else But Me,' for the two comic characters, is an amusing satire on a grand opera duet, while the 'Italian Street Song,' with its spirited, if not highly original, chorus, against arabesques of high tones for the soprano, had to be repeated four times. In the finale to this act, and in the other numbers calling for full vocal forces, Mr. Herbert's exceptionally skillful treatment of the chorus was always evident.

"The second act contains much other delightfully melodious music, its climax being reached in the 'Dream' melody, a slow waltz heard several times during the opera and reaching its finest development in a really splendid orchestral intermezzo and again in a duet for tenor and soprano. . . . The entire orchestral part is replete with felicitous touches better than anything of their kind their writer has yet done. Mr. Herbert himself wielded the baton on the first night with the result that everything went for its full value. At the close of the first act the enthusiasm was positively riotous and the principals were showered with flowers. Victor Herbert received a stormy welcome when dragged on the stage by Miss Trentini, but the audience would not calm down until Mr. Hammerstein had risen in his box to bow four or five times. He made no speech, though there were loud calls for one."

On this night, Victor Herbert reached the zenith of his career. In view of later developments, though, he would always have considered this an unfair statement.

XIV

WHILE Victor Herbert was conducting the Pittsburgh Symphony Orchestra, an incident occurred which developed into a legal action celebrated in American musical history.

The *Musical Courier* published the following editorial in its issue of July 17, 1901:

"A cablegram from London states that Victor Herbert's 'Fortune Teller' made a most lamentable failure at the Shaftesbury Theatre and that it is doubtful whether American plays would hereafter be given in that theater.

"Our standards of taste are based on European decisions and we are compelled to bow meekly to this conclusion regarding this comic opera; but it is necessary to say that this paper, the *Musical Courier*, as it is known, held not only that the 'Fortune Teller' had no merit whatever, but that all of Victor Herbert's comic operas were pure and simple plagiarisms. There is not one light aria, waltz movement, polka, gallop or march in those operas that has touched the public ear, and the street pianos have ignored them—the best evidence that the people do not find them palatable.

"The whole Sousa repertoire is alive and pulsating; the whole Herbert repertoire is stone dead, and London merely acted on rhythmic impulse when it rejected this agglomeration of puerile piracies and refused to countenance them.

"But what has all this to do with Pittsburgh? We refer our readers to an article on another page, giving some curious conditions revolving about the orchestra and Victor Herbert.

"From the very outset it could not be understood by equipoised minds how a writer of comic operas (and American comic operas, at that) and a conductor of brass bands, accustomed to parade at the head of militia and processions, could possibly be the conductor of a symphony orchestra.

"The greatest composers of classic comic operas— Offenbach, Lecocq and Von Suppe—could not have been suggested by the wildest fancy as directors of symphony concerts for the simple reason that the genre is not only distinct, but separate, and that the artistic impulse that drives a man to write 'La Grand Duchesse' or 'La Fille de Mme. Angot,' drives him out of the atmosphere of classical music.

"Everything written by Victor Herbert is copied; there is not one original strain in anything he has done, and all his copies are from sources that are comic or serio-comic. He became popular suddenly by attaining command of a brass band and joining a rollicking club of actors and Bohemians known as the Lambs, who, removed entirely from any musical comprehension, accepted the good-natured band leader as their musical dictator, and American fashion immediately paralleled him with serious-minded composers. It was never a serious matter in itself.

"How Pittsburgh intelligence could ever accept this clever bandmaster as its symphony director passes comprehension, unless, indeed, the people there never really appreciated the true significance of the artistic movement a permanent symphony orchestra represents. George H. Wilson (the manager of the orchestra) could never have had any real sympathy for the Herbert craze, for he is too deeply versed in the theory of the symphony to claim that Herbert could possibly be a permanent success as such a director. Possibly Mr. Wilson's candor finally erupted, and as a result the change is announced to which the article we print elsewhere refers.

"Custom is the forerunner of law, and in the particular field of symphony, custom has placed at its interpretative head such musicians as are only identified with the pursuit of classical music. The Leipsic Gewandhaus and Reinecke recently, who was succeeded by Nikisch; the successor in the Berlin Philharmonic to Bulow was Nikisch; Seidl succeeded Thomas here, and Baur, of the Boston Symphony, succeeded Seidl. The great symphony conductors are not drafted from the ranks of the composers of shoddy American farce opera, alias leg shows, nor are they taken from the leaders of parading military bands, who are specialists, and who develop in that direction solely.

"If Mr. Herbert were a symphony conductor he could not write the music for these American farce operas. It would be impossible; his mind would rebel and his musical constitution would protest, but as he is not, per se, a symphony conductor, he amiably drops into the condition best fitted for his mind and his æsthetics, and hence he writes 'Fortune Tellers,' 'Wizards of the Nile,' 'The Idol's Eyes,' etc., and this is the reason why he and George Wilson could not remain permanently adjusted. The dislocation was bound to come."

The other article mentioned in the above is a news story published in the *Pittsburgh Leader* which gives some sidelights on that part of Herbert's personality which was not usually disclosed to most of those who knew him. It begins:

" 'FREDERICK M. RANCKEN, MANAGER FOR VICTOR
HERBERT'S PITTSBURGH ORCHESTRA.'

"The gossips are telling how this innocent-looking caption on the letter-heads of the popular director of the Pittsburgh Symphony Orchestra is going to stir up what, in the vernacular of the street, is designated as a 'hot time' in the city's crack musical organization. The *Leader* has already printed the report that Mr. Rancken, a well-known manager of comic opera companies, and the writer of the book of Herbert's 'Ameer,' in which Frank Daniels has been starring, has been engaged to supplant George H. Wilson in the management of the Pittsburgh Orchestra's out-of-town tours, but the busybodies of the musical world look beyond the mere rumored change in the management of the concerts outside of Pittsburgh, and, per se, imagine they see the inception of a bitter internecine fight which, they predict, will either disrupt the orchestra or result in the resignation of Mr. Herbert.

"According to the official statement made by William N. Frew, chairman of the orchestra committee, when the *Leader* told him of the report from New York that Mr. Rancken was to succeed Mr. Wilson as manager of the orchestra, Mr. Wilson was reëlected manager of the orchestra some time ago and will serve until next March at least. Unofficially, it is said, that the real trouble may develop into a contest between Mr. Herbert and Mr. Frew, the latter having taken up the cudgels on behalf of Mr. Wilson. Some misunderstandings between the orchestra director and the manager occurred last season in regard to railroad arrangements for the tours and this is made the excuse for the employment of Mr. Rancken who, so the story goes, is to stay in Pittsburgh during the season and collaborate with Mr. Herbert in the writing of several new operas. . . .

"When the report became known, however, that a Wood Street printing house had been given an order to print a quantity of letterheads for Mr. Herbert with the name of Mr. Rancken and the title of business manager of 'Victor Herbert's Pittsburgh Orchestra' following it, there were those who foresaw dire things for the symphony orchestra. . . ."

If the great Toscanini himself were to print letterheads reading, "Toscanini's Philharmonic Orchestra,"

Rehearsing "Madeleine" at the Metropolitan.
Victor Herbert and Frances Alda Are Seated.

"DO WRITE A SONG FOR US MR HERBERT!"

this would be considered a bit of startling presumption. It would be similarly regarded if the orchestra were a lesser organization than the Philharmonic. Yet Herbert had no hesitancy in seizing an opportunity to subordinate the symphonic organization of Pittsburgh to himself.

He did the same thing not long after he took over Gilmore's Band, calling it "Victor Herbert's Twenty-second Regiment Band, formerly Gilmore's," and when he left Pittsburgh and organized his own orchestra, it was, of course, "Victor Herbert's New York Orchestra"; not "The New York Orchestra, directed by Victor Herbert."

Herbert was always the showman and the actor; his name had to lead.

The *Musical Courier* article was written by Marc A. Blumenberg, the editor of the journal. Blumenberg was a dynamic individual who possessed an acute wish for power, a good knowledge of and taste for music, the ability to express himself with vitriolic forcefulness when necessary, and a front-page fearlessness, whether he was right or wrong.

He was unpopular with musicians, not only because of his sharp tongue and pen, but because his methods often were based on the premise that in a magazine all roads should lead to advertising. When this résumé of Herbert's talents therefore appeared, the news of it spread like a prairie fire.

Herbert was roused to wild anger and brought suit against the paper for fifty thousand dollars, alleging libel. Although he took exception to all of Blumenberg's statements the matter soon settled down to the charge of plagiarism. Thus did the musical *cause célèbre* begin.

The case was tried in the New York Supreme Court, starting October 22, 1902. The scene was set against a background of antagonism toward Blumenberg. Almost every music artist was either openly or secretly glad to see the *Courier's* editor in the rôle of defendant.

Blumenberg's counsel was the celebrated Abe Hummel. The clever little lawyer's strategy was to show that the *Courier's* editorial was to be classed as ordinary criticism; that it was justifiable for a music critic to say that a composer's work was not original, but adapted from other music. Hummel also wanted to bring the jury to the state of mind where they would think that, because Herbert led a band, and also composed comic operas, he did not have that artistic consciousness found in acknowledged classical composers. He wanted them to believe that because Herbert wrote mainly to order that his works were insincere and unworthy.

Herbert's lawyer, Arthur C. Palmer, set himself a clear course. It was his contention that to call a man a plagiarist was not criticism, but libel.

When Herbert was on the witness stand, Justice Truax, who presided, asked him the odd question:

"Were your operas pure and simple plagiarism?"

Of course Herbert found it simple to answer:

"They were not."

Then Hummel asked him if he had not been the

leader of the Twenty-second Regimental *Brass* Band. Herbert indignantly retorted that it was not a brass band, but a regimental band.

The word, "orchestrate," came up, and so much time was taken up in explaining the difference between "orchestrating" and an "orchestration" that the jury became dizzy. This discussion grew out of the testimony of a witness who said he had made an orchestration of Herbert's music, meaning he had adapted a Herbert score for some group of instruments. Hummel wanted to prove that this meant the witness had orchestrated Herbert's music, a fact which would have inferred that Herbert could not do such work himself.

So the case went on, swamped in much foolishness and many irrelevancies. Herbert was steadfast in saying that he had not written for money, even if all his operettas were contracted for. He declared he did not receive any money in advance of writing his scores.

The defense had compiled a number of excerpts from Herbert's works to prove his alleged plagiarisms, but in most cases they were vague and far-fetched. In one instance, the defense had even rewritten a phrase from Beethoven in order to make it conform to a Herbert passage.

One or two pieces, however, did show a strong resemblance to something else. But such evidence was neutralized when Walter Damrosch was put on the stand to testify for Herbert.

Damrosch was Herbert's most important witness. The opposing testimony thinned and evaporated against his words. But in testifying he made some strange statements. For example, when the defense showed similarity between a Herbert waltz and a Waldteufel waltz, he said:

"Composers of waltzes are bound by certain definite limitations, which must make necessary some like points in their composition. The first few notes are similar . . . but to say that this constitutes copying, is absurd and nonsensical."

He repeated this opinion several times, and then laid down the amazing axiom that the beginning of a composition is a pure formalism and practically common property.

"It is," he declared, "as if I were to begin a fairy tale by saying: 'Once upon a time there lived . . .' "

This idea caught the judge's fancy and traveled to the jury.

The defense was endeavoring to show that the openings of several Herbert pieces were similar to the openings of other pieces. It is a fact known to any musician that compositions, no matter what their length, are inspired by themes of only a few notes, and that, in numerous cases, these themes come at the very beginning of the music. To say therefore, as Damrosch did, that the opening of a composition may be considered as inconsequential introductory matter was entirely wrong.

But neither the judge, the jury, or Hummel had much musical understanding, and the *Courier's* witnesses were mostly obscure people who were not of much help to Blumenberg. The testimony of Damrosch carried the greatest weight. After being out but a short time, the jury found a verdict for Herbert, awarding him fifteen thousand dollars.

The *Courier* deserved defeat because of Blumenberg's truly poisonous statements. But it might have made a better showing had the case been better prepared.

After the trial, Hummel met Damrosch in the hall. Damrosch had been warned that Hummel would make it hard for him on the witness stand. To his surprise, he had found the lawyer most courteous and considerate. So he said:

"You were very gentle with me, Mr. Hummel."

"How could I help it when my sister is one of your greatest admirers?" the lawyer replied.

Herbert was now a hero. He had beaten Marc Blumenberg. Joyous over the outcome, he gave a dinner at Lüchow's to his friends and to those who had aided him at the trial. He presented Damrosch with a book, in manuscript, of his orchestral arrangements of small pieces.

The *Courier* appealed the verdict. Nine months later the Appellate Division sustained the verdict, but cut the amount of damages down to $5,185.45. It also ruled that if Herbert was dissatisfied with this amount the case should be retried.

The excitement this affair created among New York musicians, and the animosities it uncovered, is pictured by the English vocal teacher and critic, Herman Klein.

He found himself, a bewildered stranger, unexpectedly involved in the situation. Klein wrote in his autobiography, "Musicians and Mummers":

"Only in retrospect can one perceive how incidents, apparently insignificant at the time they occur, can influence for good or harm the whole course of subsequent events.

"Most people by now have, I daresay, entirely forgotten the name of the clever man who founded, and for many years edited, the New York *Musical Courier*. Marc Blumenberg was a typical American of Teutonic-Jewish descent, smart, subtle, adroit, a man of powerful intellect, concealing under his engaging *bonhomie* an inflexible policy and iron will. I had met him in London through Percy Betts, the musical critic of the *Daily News*.

"Towards the end of 1902, Marc Blumenberg was mulcted by a New York court in very heavy damages for a libelous criticism in his paper concerning the well-known light-opera composer, Victor Herbert. So much I had heard before leaving England. I was not aware, however, that friends of Victor Herbert had arranged to hold a banquet on some date in January, 1903, to celebrate his signal victory over the hated editor of the *Musical Courier*. On the first day I called at his office, Blumenberg asked me if I had been invited to this dinner. I told him I had not.

" 'Would you go if you were asked?'

" 'I don't think so. I don't know Victor Herbert, and I fail to see that the affair concerns me in any way.'

[190]

" 'Perhaps not. But you must understand that if you are not present you will be looked upon as a friend and supporter of the *Courier,* and that means high treason against Victor Herbert and the Damrosches and the rest of them.'

" 'But why can't I be neutral? I have only just arrived in New York and there is no reason why I should take sides in a quarrel of this sort. I may never be invited.'

" 'Well,' said Marc Blumenberg, 'if you do go, I shall of course know, and I warn you that in this matter the motto of both parties is, "Those not with me are against me?" ' And I left his office with that menace ringing in my ears.

"A few days later the banquet took place and I thought I was safe, for no request to attend or support it had reached me. Nevertheless, the repercussion was to come. The next issue of the *Musical Courier* contained, almost side by side with a satirical account of the feast, a long interview with myself dealing purely with vocal questions. This, I imagine, drew special attention to my absence from the banquet, and the inevitable happened: I became a marked man. Thenceforward, to the day I left New York for good, seven years later, I was unable to count as a real friend any one of the musicians who had taken sides with Victor Herbert."

Herbert won his suit—but the case cannot be dismissed as completely as the jury dismissed it. The examples of plagiarism which Blumenberg served up in court, and the witnesses he summoned as experts, were most ineffectual.

Maurice S. Richter, a play broker, has an odd story to tell apropos of the question of Herbert's plagiarism. He says:

"About nine years ago, I was working for the Fox Film Company. I had written some poems which a number of prominent men of letters had liked, and I thought that Victor Herbert might be interested in setting them to music. I telephoned Mr. Herbert, and through my picture connection I was granted an appointment. He read my poems and commended them very highly. But he regretted his inability to write the music because of lack of time. He told me he was under contract to a motion picture concern—the name of which I don't recall—to write scores for several feature photoplays, and for that reason it was impossible for him to engage in outside work.

"When I asked his advice he suggested that I go to any good musician and ask him to adapt some well-known classical tunes to my poems. He told me that he himself had borrowed a great deal of material from the masters, and used this material as the basic melodies for many of his popular successes.

"Our conversation took place in Herbert's home. I remember it as an elaborately furnished room with an expensive Persian rug, a grand piano, a bookcase and with paintings on the wall.

"I don't know why he should have particularized in his advice as he did, except that he said my lyrics were not suitable for jazz music. I left in amazement at his suggestion, for he was perfectly serious."

Later, when this story was brought to the attention of Alice Nielsen, she, too, had a further comment to make.

"I now recall something that happened during the run of 'The Serenade'," she said. "I was then very inexperienced, musically, and knew little of the literature of music. Our musical director, Paul Steindorff, interested himself in me and undertook to coach me in some of the soprano rôles of grand opera.

"One day we were in the theatre, going through some music at the piano. I was singing an aria from an opera. I can't remember which opera it was, but I do know that it was one of the standard ones. The aria had a cadenza, and when I came to it, I stopped and exclaimed indignantly: 'Why, that man has stolen Victor's cadenza!'

"The cadenza was practically the same as the one in 'The Serenade,' and in my ignorance, I thought that the master who composed the opera had written it after Herbert composed his work. Steindorff agreed that the two cadenzas were similar."

Between 1893 and 1895, Isaac Albeniz, the famous Spanish composer, wrote a set of five "Songs of Spain" for the piano. One of them is titled, "Cordoba." In 1905, Victor Herbert wrote "Kiss Me Again" for Mlle. Modiste. Here are the main themes from the two compositions:

CORDOBA

KISS ME AGAIN

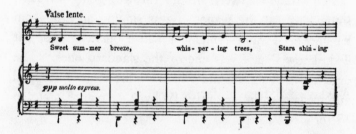

The melodies are practically similar, even to the trill on the first note of the third measure. The only pronounced difference is that the Albeniz piece is written in the minor. Nor does the strange resemblance end with the music. Albeniz has a foreword to "Cordoba," reading:

> "The silence of the night, where naught was heard but
> the murmur of jasmine-scented breezes, is invaded by
> the sound of the guzlas accompanying serenades and
> thrilling the air with ardent melodies and tones soft as
> the swaying of the palms high overhead."

[194]

The words of "Kiss Me Again" begin:

> "Sweet summer breeze,
> Whispering trees,
> Stars shining softly above . . ."

Herbert did not set his melody to Blossom's lyric, in which case the resemblance might be put down to uncanny coincidence. He wrote the music first, and then gave it to his librettist to add the words.

There are many passages in the Herbert scores which are so reminiscent that the listener involuntarily and abruptly stops to ask: "Where did I hear that?"

Not all these passages are so distinctly familiar that the source can be traced. One begins by wondering where a certain melodic strain comes from, wanders off into tributaries, and ends by being frankly puzzled.

For example, take Cleopatra's solo, "I Have Been A-Maying," from "The Wizard of the Nile":

I HAVE BEEN A-MAYING

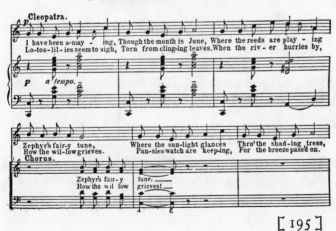

and compare it with the "Barcarolle," and "The Legend of the Bells," from Planquette's operetta, "The Chimes of Normandy," a previous work:

BARCAROLLE

LEGEND OF THE BELLS

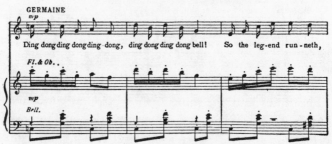

There is no positive similarity and Planquette could not win a case against Herbert in any court. Yet the resemblance is there, with the inference that one influenced the other.

Take some more decided examples:

One of the standard Herbert melodies is the "Serenade," written in his early days. This is the motif:

SERENADE

Now compare it with the opening phrase of Schubert's song, "Heiden-Röslein."

HEIDEN-RÖSLEIN

The notes and the time of the first two measures of both melodies are the same, except that in Herbert's piece there are two quarter notes in the first measure instead of four eighths, and the notes of the second bar an eighth and two sixteenths instead of four sixteenths.

In "Babes in Toyland," there is a song, "Barney O'Flynn." The refrain goes:

BARNEY O'FLYNN

In Thomas's opera, "Mignon," the well-known aria, "Dost Thou Know That Fair Land?" has this phrase, which is one of the leading passages (at "I fain would live—"):

DOST THOU KNOW THAT FAIR LAND

18470

Both compositions are in the same time, practically the same key (D major and D flat major), and the tonal progression is sufficiently the same to make the similarity inescapable.

Finally, "The Stone-Cutters' Song" from "The Wizard of the Nile":

STONE-CUTTERS' SONG

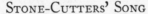

and Handel's famous melody, "The Harmonious Blacksmith":

THE HARMONIOUS BLACKSMITH

Here, too, the likeness is not only in the music, but also in the intent of both compositions.

These few examples are not at all the result of a deliberate hunt for similarities. They were merely noted as some Herbert passage recalled another melody.

Sam Finkelstein, one of the leading players in the Pittsburgh Orchestra, and later with Herbert's operetta orchestras, admits that resemblances in Herbert's music were often commented upon by the men in the orchestras. He recalls hearing one of them caustically remark: "Whenever I hear a new Herbert composition I think he comes pretty near."

Finkelstein declares that Herbert was rather sensitive on the point.

"He had a marvelous memory for melodies," the musician recalls, "and once he heard a piece he never forgot it. Frequently, when he wrote a new composition, he would ask me, anxiously: 'Where does it come from?'"

What is the meaning of these similarities? What does such a clear likeness as exists between "Cordoba" and "Kiss Me Again" mean? Did Victor Herbert deliberately help himself to the music of other composers on occasion? Or did he unconsciously reproduce existing compositions?

Since he wrote so many good melodies of undoubted originality, the supposition must be that these adaptations were unconscious. But even so, with his long memory and his musicianship, he could not help but notice the resemblance after a composition was written.

[200]

Page from the Manuscript of "A Suite of Serenades,"
Victor Herbert's Contribution to Paul Whiteman's
Concert of "Symphonic Jazz."

Autographed Title Page of Herbert's "Suite Romantique."
The quotation is the love theme from "Hero and Leander."

Why, then, did he let it go?   Perhaps because he was a careless man in music, and prodigiously prolific.

He must brusquely have told himself that there were only a couple of similar bars in a composition several pages long. The development was his own, so what did it matter?

XV

During the years after his return from Pittsburgh, when Victor Herbert was turning out a comic opera on an average of every five months, he was also busily engaged in keeping up with what, through usage and necessity, is called "serious" music.

He organized "Victor Herbert's New York Orchestra," which gave Sunday concerts in theaters during the winter, and played seasonal engagements at summer parks, mainly at Saratoga Springs, New York, and at Willow Grove Park, in Pennsylvania.

A Pittsburgh journalist visited Herbert in 1904, and wrote for his paper a detailed description of the composer and his home in New York at that time:

"Mr. Herbert is carving a name for himself. He has made a great many friends in the six months of his residence here. He lives at 866 West End Avenue. This is regarded as uptown. It is but a step from the subway station, which is labelled 'One Hundred and Third Street.' But the subway whizzes you at the rate of about twenty miles an hour and the uptown portion of New York is very easy of access.

"Mr. Herbert's home is in the residence portion of the city, is one of a row of houses, and is about four stories high. The interior is much the same as the great composer's former home on Aikens Avenue, Pittsburgh. The exterior is of light sandstone. There is no yard in front and but a few trees. . . .

"Mr. Herbert's workshop is on the second floor front and it is there that he is writing the four or five operas for which he now has contracts. These operas will be produced during the coming year and Mr. Herbert thinks they are superior to anything he has yet done. The composer is always striving for betterment in music and expects some day to write the great American opera, which he will probably do.

"There is an air of comfort and simplicity about Mr. Herbert's working room. In one corner, near a door, stands the grand piano on which he runs over his score. Near a window and within easy reach of the instrument, is a high desk similar to that used by bookkeepers but much shorter. Here, perched on a high stool, working away at a score, Mr. Herbert was found by the writer. His first queries were about Pittsburgh. He wanted to know how his old friends were, what they were doing, and was sincerely anxious to know if the Pittsburgh Symphony Orchestra and his friend, Emil Pauer, were being properly patronized. On being assured of their success, Mr. Herbert was genuinely pleased.

" 'I still have a warm feeling for the city of Pittsburgh and its people,' said Mr. Herbert. 'The good old smoky town was my home for several years, and one of the greatest sources of regret of my life was when business and other considerations caused me to sever my connection with the Pittsburgh Orchestra. I was highly gratified at the reception I received during my engagement with the orchestra during the Exposition, and I hope to renew all my old friendships in your city when next I appear there with my orchestra.'

"Mr. Herbert referred modestly to the success of his orchestra at the Majestic Theatre, in New York. Yet others, not personally interested, told the writer that the Sunday night concerts of Victor Herbert have caught on, and that large crowds of music lovers fill the theatre every Sunday night. Mr. Herbert's idea of giving New York a composition by one of the greatest living composers that it has never heard before is attracting attention. This novelty first aroused the interest of New Yorkers, then their enthusiasm, and now there is no doubt of the organization's success. Along about Easter the orchestra will start on a road tour, embracing most of the cities formerly visited by Herbert at the head of the Pittsburgh Orchestra.

"Mr. Herbert has four new operas in the making and another under contract. He is enthusiastic about writing the music and enjoys the hard work which the composition of several operas demands. One of the most recent happenings which pleases him is the coming revival of his opera, 'Babette,' in which is contained some of his most pretentious music. This opera was written for Fritzi Scheff, the piquant little grand opera singer, and some of the numbers given her in that piece are thought to be the best Mr. Herbert has ever written. The piece was proclaimed a success. Everything looked rosy for the opera until Charles B. Dillingham, a young man in the theatrical business who was Miss

Scheff's business manager, decided the public did not like her songs and made up his mind to take it off. Against the wishes of Victor Herbert, 'Babette' was closed, and 'Two Roses,' by Ludwig Englander, substituted. This was short-lived and Miss Scheff fell back to Von Suppe's 'Fatinitza,' which she is now playing in New York pending the revival of 'Babette.' "

The class of compositions Herbert played at his Sunday concerts may be estimated from a ballot he took when he announced he would give a request program. Herbert numbers were named on almost every ballot, the favorites being selections from "It Happened in Nordland," "Babes in Toyland," and "Babette." Other requests were for the overture from "Poet and Peasant." Next came Rossini's "William Tell" overture, the introduction to the third act of "Lohengrin," the march from Raff's "Lenore" symphony, Rubenstein's "Melody in F," and Massenet's "Scenes Neapolitans."

Herbert made some strange remarks about these requests in a little article he wrote for an American musical magazine:

"Recently I gave a request program at the Majestic where the numbers on the card were made up from the letters received. While it was gratifying for me to note that my own compositions were most frequently requested (perhaps because the writers wanted to be nice), yet the requests for the great composers were so numerous as to indicate that there is no decadence in popular taste, but rather a change for the better, which was so palpably evident to me that I turned to my manager, Mr. W. V. Clayton, and said: 'Clayton, this is a music-loving community and it is as different to-day from what it was when I came here twenty years ago as is day from night. Listen to the applause which greets a Haydn symphony to-day. Twenty years ago it would have been received in silence.'"

With all his association with musical masterpieces under Seidl, Thomas, and with European orchestras, he could still call the music of the request programs, "great." With the exception of the "Lohengrin" prelude, they are little better than parlor music.

This was in 1905. In the same year the Philharmonic Society paid its respects to Herbert by engaging him to conduct two sets of concerts in December and March. He was one of no less than six conductors who led the Philharmonic men that season, the others being Willem Mengelberg, Wassily Safonoff, Ernst Kunwald, Max Fiedler, and Fritz Steinbach.

At the first concert, Herbert conducted the Dvorák "New World Symphony," Grieg's "Piano Concert in A minor," with Raoul Pugno as soloist, Schubert's "Theme and Variations from the String Quartet in D minor," and Liszt's "Les Preludes." At the second concert Raff's "In Walde" symphony, and Beethoven's violin concerto in D major, played by Henri Marteau, and Herbert's "Suite Romantique" were performed. The latter work was composed in 1900 for, and dedicated to, the Pittsburgh Orchestra, which played it for the first time on February 2, of the same year. New

York heard it on February 26, when the Pittsburgh organization gave a concert in Carnegie Hall.

An official description of the suite was prepared under Herbert's direction for the Pittsburgh Orchestra's program notes. It is a long, detailed scenario, and a rather curious document, considering that the composer had a hand in its writing:

"The first movement, 'Visions,' in A major, consists of an exposition and Allegro. The rhythmically strong subject—only a few bars—with which the work begins, may be taken as its motto. It is like a joyous outburst, a tribute to love. After a pianissimo leading comes a theme, first in the strings, expressive of longing, and suggesting the title of the movement. It is suddenly interrupted by the motto, as if confident, strongly scored and is used in the working up to the entrance of the main portion of the movement, allegro appassionata. The principal theme of this part is given out by violas, cellos, clarinets and bassoons, accompanied by an impassioned triplet movement in the upper strings. The first violins afterwards take it up gently. As it is continued by the violins, the horns and then the woodwind choir take up the restless rhythm of the motto as an accompaniment. Now the composer proceeds to develop the main theme, using in connection with it the two ideas heard in the exposition portion. The attentive hearer will note that the principal theme of the allegro is used as a support to the 'Longing' motive given out by the strings. Much variety of color appears here. The mood, generally pensive, is suddenly interrupted by the motto, this time more strenuously stated. . . ."

There is more, and still more, of this. It is like the eager outpourings of a man who has felt himself restricted and takes full advantage of an opportune outlet for assertion. Herbert had gained success in comic opera—yes. But he wanted recognition as an inhabitant of that Parnassus called serious music. Thus the careful elaboration of a composition which could not rise above its composer's true metier—the operetta stage.

Musical America gave the accepted criticism of the suite in this paragraph:

"It is a strange mixture of elements, consisting of certain commonplaces endowed with much orchestral color. It is this orchestral brilliancy which is most to be admired in it, and which predominated in the playing of the Philharmonic."

Herbert's opinions on music were in consonance with the work he did. He was always ready to express himself, and did, on many occasions. Perhaps those opinions are best crystallized in an intelligent and authoritative interview published in the *New York Sun*, December 9, 1906. He said then:

"If you can only make a thing popular your path is easy, and to make anything popular you must study the popular need.

"In regard to music, we only love what we understand, we cannot love what we do not understand. I mean this superficial statement to refer to the great masses of people who have only time in their crowded lives to yield occasionally to their impulses to hear some good music and who cannot in those rare moments rise and fall to the heights and depths of emotion and understanding demanded by great compositions like those of Bach, Liszt, et al., but who really want good music and respond when you give it to them with their patronage and applause.

"They don't want cheap music, but they want something delicate, pretty, graceful, sensuous, but not hypersensuous. The masses who approach every domain of art unbiased by technique make that same demand everywhere—the light touch—and the artist who desires to answer that need must give what is wanted."

That is the unconscious defense of one who jealously aspired to a place beyond his natural level in the musical world; in it is plainly to be seen the man who always had the audience clearly before him.

He goes on further to reveal himself:

"The rôle of being serious is demanded often by a hypocritical world which mistakes seriousness for development, evolution, all the things that it is not. It is the easiest thing in the world to be serious, but to be nothing else—that is an anchor to inspiration, a deterioration instead of a progress in art. To take a serious subject and to so adorn it with the flower of fancy that you attract the most hidebound—is not that an achievement? I think so.

"Shakespeare never wrote a play into which he did not introduce a low-comedy rôle. 'Hamlet' is serious enough, that no one will dispute, and in no play is there any greater farce than in the famous graveyard scene of that tragedy.

"Even Beethoven had moments of musical comedy. If he lost a penny he would sit down and compose a rondo and call it, 'The Rage for a Lost Coin,' which, in German, sounds rather appalling.

"Every artist recognizes the law of contrast, which is one of the fundamental rules of composition, whether it be literary or musical or made with brush and canvas. The program for one of the most popular concerts I conducted recently is like the menu for a dinner, from soup to nuts. There must be contrast, something to appeal to every taste. You can't serve all lamb chops any more than you can serve an entire bill of fare made up of froths and frills.

"The popularity of my concerts has pleased me immensely, for it has proved that I have succeeded in doing what I have crudely outlined in this talk; and besides that I recognize the fact that their popularity means more than they would if they were subsidized, as most of the musical organizations here have to be."

It is a pathetic confession.

In another article, signed by himself, he expressed similar thoughts:

"To be regretted is the fact that a few of our leading composers are so little known. But they do not approach their public on level ground. They remain too far removed; too distant to feel the popular pulse. To many of them the word, 'popular,' is a fetich, yet their works, often of rare beauty and merit, almost invariably fail of a wide appeal because of a sincere but misguided idea of what their audiences desire. That time has passed when intelligent persons are content with any work, music or literature, of which they are forced to remark: 'Yes, it is very beautiful, indeed, although I do not understand all of it.'

"Personally I hold that that which is not 'popular' is not of much benefit to the world."

Herbert's words are both a confession and somewhat of an indictment of himself. They will probably make artists shudder with resentment.

XVI

In 1907, Oscar Hammerstein signed a contract with
Herbert for an "American grand opera," to be produced the following season. This was the origin of
"Natoma," but some dramatic musical history was to
occur before it was heard by an opera public.

Hammerstein wanted an American novelty for his
Manhattan Opera House. He wanted it more for the
advertising possibilities than because of any genuine
belief in the possible merits of such a work. With his
customary theatricality, he had a lot to say about the
projected opera. First:

"The way to get a libretto is to ask for it and pay
for it. So I offer a thousand dollars to the man, pref-
erably an American, who will provide a suitable libretto
for Victor Herbert."

And then:

"Now that I have decided to give an opera by an
American composer, you may be certain that such an
opera will be given every opportunity and every advantage. I shall devote to it the best orchestra pro-
curable and the best singers in my company, among
whom is that supreme artiste, Lillian Nordica. And
when I have finally produced it, I shall have broken
the record in novelty-giving."

The story of "Natoma" has to do with an Indian girl, its main character. Read then, what Herbert had to say of Indians in opera when he signed the Hammerstein contract:

"I should like to have an American subject and a background of American romance, though, contrary to what many suppose, the terms of Mr. Hammerstein's generous offer of a thousand dollars for the best libretto do not expressly stipulate an American subject. The preference is mentioned, but the hard and fast condition is not made.

"If the subject be an American one it is not absolutely necessary that the *dramatis personae* be either Indians or Puritans. Indians are not a suitable subject for an opera. The state of the Indians is pathetic, it is true, but in an opera they would not exactly strike audiences seriously. You will see what I mean:

"Suppose an Indian tenor, taking a high C and then trilling on a high D in order to touch the emotions of a sopranofied prima donna squaw! The taste and sense balk at such things!"

"Natoma" made use of Indian musical themes. In the same outline of his opera plans, Herbert said:

"An American atmosphere is not obtained by pepper-casting the score with themes from patriotic songs. Puccini, in 'Madame Butterfly,' makes use of 'The Star Spangled Banner,' for instance, and also of a few Japanese harmonies. Does that make his opera American, Japanese, or even a mixture of both?

[213]

"If I wanted to point out something vitally and poetically American in music, I should point to that movement in Dvorák's beautiful symphony, 'From the New World,' wherein he depicts in passages of extraordinary poetry and sustained beauty the musical feelings aroused in him by the idea of the vast expanse of starlit, wind-swept prairie."

Herbert once had a furious argument with the critic, Henry T. Finck, about this practice of injecting folk-themes into compositions. He told Finck he had little regard for the music of Grieg because the latter availed himself of national tunes.

The search for the great American libretto went on, and meanwhile Herbert continued on the serious side of music with his orchestral concerts. The Sunday concerts, many of them given at the Broadway Theatre, were well attended. This was as much due to the popularity of the composer as to the light nature of his programs. Victor Herbert was the only man in older New York musical history who gave such concerts successfully.

During the winter seasons his orchestra was engaged for various private functions and benefits. At one of these he made a humorous pun on a grim word. He was playing at a benefit for the Anti-Vivisection Society at the Waldorf-Astoria. Before beginning the concert, Herbert rapped on his stand and addressed his men:

"Gentlemen, in view of the nature of the association under whose auspices this afternoon's entertainment is to be held, there will be no cuts in the music of the program."

He was active, too, in helping to safeguard the copyright interests of American musicians. They were in danger because phonograph and player-piano companies were attempting to have a law passed exempting mechanically recorded music from copyright fees. Herbert was president of the "Authors and Composers Copyright Association"—the parent body of the present "American Society of Authors and Composers"—and led a committee to Washington to fight for a law protecting composers. He issued many statements to arouse the public interest. One of them has a biographical interest:

". . . They (the companies) pay Caruso a vast retainer to sing into their records; they pay him as high as a dollar a disc royalty besides, and charge six dollars for the disc. On the other hand, Puccini, or any other composer of the music Caruso sings, gets nothing for the use of his music. . . . Another thing, they of necessity give abbreviated and mutilated versions of every composition they play. Take, for instance, my 'American Fantasy.' That, as I have written it, should take twenty or twenty-five minutes to play, and the poetic idea I have tried to express, the effect I have tried to create, is dependent upon the arrangement of the patriotic airs. Necessarily, they have cut it on a disc requiring four or five minutes in its playing and the consequence is that the piece is slashed and ruined out of all semblance of its former real state. I can say to any manager to whom I sell a piece of music: 'It must be played or sung thus or so,' and my request is regarded or he doesn't get the music; but I have no say-so with the men who send my compositions broadcast through the country."

Later, Victor Herbert's income was to be amplified greatly through records made of his music and of his orchestra, and of music played by the studio orchestras under his conductorship.

By the time the libretto for Herbert's grand opera was found and the music written, Oscar Hammerstein's operatic ventures were turning out badly. He had incurred the enmity of certain social leaders, and their withdrawal of patronage, together with his lack of a substantial subscription list, had put the balance of his fight with the Metropolitan against him.

Under such circumstances, Oscar was unwilling to risk the production of "Natoma," which evidently did not appeal to him as promising success. He gave Herbert the excuse that the opera was "too late," and the composer was left with the work of a year on his hands.

The libretto was written by Joseph D. Redding, a San Francisco lawyer, musician and author. Redding was the first president of the famous Bohemian Club, of San Francisco. He was also the writer of some of the pageants which this organization gave in the open air among the giant redwoods of the California forests.

He provided Herbert with a melodramatic tale of love and intrigue revolving around an Indian girl in the early days of California. This Indian maiden was somewhat akin to "Aïda," and Herbert must have been attracted to the story for that reason. There was also some opportunity for Spanish music, which surely recalled to Herbert the blandishments of "Carmen."

At any rate, he was satisfied with the libretto, and thus placed himself in the unique position of being the only one who was.

"Natoma" contains such gems of lyricism as:

> "Gentle maiden, tell me,
>> Have I seen thee in my dreams,
>> I wonder?
> When above my pillow,
>> From the night fell starry gleams,
>> I wonder?
> Ever am I haunted
>> By a pair of eyes so deep
>> And gleaming,
> In whose wealth unfathomed,
>> Lie the shafts of love asleep
>> And dreaming."

And:

> "Ah, bid me now, when none can hear,
> To whisper in thy kindly ear,
> The greatest story ever told,
> A story new and never old."

Or lines like these:

Natoma: "Oh, Paul, take me, beat me, kill me, but let me be your slave!"
Paul: "You little wild flower!"

And these climactic examples:

SERENADE
(Alvarado, in the first act)
"When the sunlight dies,
When the night-wind sighs,
When the dove is asleep in the tree;
I will come, my love,
With stars above,
To pay homage, fair cousin, to thee.

Oh, my lady love, my lady love,
Leave me not in the dusk to repine;
Oh, my lady love, my lady love,
Bid me sing to thy beauty divine."

LOVE DUET
(Close of first act)
"I love thee!
In secret hear my vow,
I love thee!
For none shall know but thou—
I love thee!
Ah, chide me not, I pray,
I love thee!
'Tis all my heart can say—
I love thee!
May heaven hear my prayer!
Beneath the stars I swe-ar!
With all my soul I love thee!"

It is difficult to understand how any composer, writing a serious opera, could set to music such unbelievably putrid verse as:

"May heaven hear my prayer!
Beneath the stars I swear!"

Any Broadway tunester would think twice before committing his music to such words. That Herbert accepted these lyrics could only indicate that he was completely indifferent to literary values—or that he lacked discrimination.

Not only are the lyrics of "Natoma" abominable, but in some cases Herbert set them unsuitably. One of the best pieces in the opera is a boat song, sung by female voices. The words are:

> "Afloat, afloat, afloat in our open boat,
>   We swing on the evening tide."

They are bad enough, but Herbert placed the accent on *a*-float, and gave a drop of six notes from the *"a"* to the *"float,"* thereby distorting the line.

Redding must be credited, however, with giving Herbert two Indian themes for the opera, one of them being the now well-known "Dagger Dance."

After Hammerstein rejected "Natoma," Herbert took it to Gatti-Casazza, of the Metropolitan, who also refused it. The opera finally was accepted by Andreas Dippel, the director of the Chicago Opera Company, which also gave performances in Philadelphia.

The première took place at the Philadelphia Metropolitan Opera House, on February 23, 1911, with the following notable cast:

Don Francisco...........Gustave Huberdau
Father Peralta...........Hector Dufranne
Alvarado...............Mario Sammarco
Castro...................Frank Preisch

[219]

Pico. Armand Crabbe
Kagama. . . . . Constantin Nicolay
Paul. . . . . John McCormack
Barbara. . . . . Lillian Grenville
Natoma. . . . . Mary Garden
Conductor. . . . . Cleofonte Campanini

It was received with such enthusiastic approbation
that Dippel took the opera forthwith to New York,
where it was given on February 28, at the Metropolitan. The reaction of the audience was thus recorded
by *Musical America:*

"Natoma . . . was granted a verdict which, if not
overwhelmingly so, was nevertheless in its favor. Long
before the opening hour the last seat in the house had
been disposed of. The boxes of the grand tier were
draped with national colors, as they had been for the
two other premières of this season, and the foyer was
decorated with greens. Programs with special covers
once more served to impart an atmosphere of uncon-
ventionality to the occasion. As for the audience, it
was of unexampled brilliancy.

"The opera had not proceeded far before there were
outbursts of applause which were, however, promptly
hissed down. Mary Garden was given a warm reception when she first appeared and another outburst
followed her delivery of 'Natoma's' narrative. Then
the audience quieted until Mr. Sammarco had sung the
love song—the most long-breathed melody of the whole
act—when there came another volley. At the fall of
the curtain there was applause which, if not the most

vociferous, was sufficient to bring the singers before the curtain nine times. It was evident that every one wanted Mr. Herbert to show himself but the curtain was finally lowered without his having appeared.

"It was not long after it started that it became plain that the second act had 'caught on.' The brilliant colors, the life and bustle, provided an element of striking contrast to the rather slow-moving first act. There was a positive uproar after Mr. Crabbe's song—with chorus—'Vaqueros, devil may care!'—a tuneful number in Mr. Herbert's most approved comic opera style. Despite the desperate efforts of the singers and of Mr. Campanini to the contrary, the house held up the proceedings until it had to be repeated. The succeeding habanera and minuet pleased, and so did Mr. McCormack's air glorifying Columbus. The climax, however, was reached in the weirdly effective 'Dagger Dance,' performed with gripping dramatic force by Miss Garden and Mr. Frank Preisch. There was a veritable storm of enthusiasm when the act ended. This time Miss Garden rushed out and soon returned, bringing to the stage Mr. Herbert and Joseph Redding, the librettist, while the audience cheered. Again and again they were recalled and with them presently appeared Mr. Campanini, Mr. Dippel, Franz Almanz, the stage director, and also the chorus master. Wreaths and bouquets of all sizes were showered upon them.

"The last act was well received, especially the orchestral introduction. The English enunciation of all, save the foreign artists who were manifestly embarrassed by their brief acquaintance with the language, was surprisingly good, and necessitated no undue strain to catch every few words. The chorus, however, was less happy in this matter. Miss Garden has done few things better than 'Natoma.' . . ."

But whatever the audience thought, the critics were little pleased. They liked parts of the Herbert score, and on the whole considered it a worth-while effort; but they generally agreed that "Natoma" was not a work to take its place in the operatic repertoire. The noted critic, Lawrence Gilman, perhaps summed up his colleagues' thoughts in this excerpt from a review he wrote for *Harper's Weekly*:

" 'Natoma' leaves no positive impression on the mind. It lacks individuality, originality and ideas—and no music has value unless it possesses at least one of these merits. In melodic style it seldom rises above the better class of salon music; it does, in Natoma's 'Hawk Song,' and in certain other passages where Mr. Herbert has used effects that are characteristic of Indian idioms. But it is a different and less admirable style of melody than he usually employs—a style that is fairly represented by the setting of Paul's fatuous 'Gentle Maiden' address of the first act.

"In harmony Mr. Herbert employs the typical modern *clichés* with dexterity and generally with aptness. . . . His instrumentation is rich and sonorous—here again we encounter the conventional modern idioms, manipulated effectively but without subtlety or imagination.

"In short, Mr. Herbert says nothing that has not been said before. By this I do not mean to imply that he has definitely reproduced the thoughts of other men; I mean simply that there is nothing new, nothing arresting, nothing distinguished, in his handling of the elements of musical expression that are available to the opera maker of to-day. Native skill and a sense of theatrical effect, supported by adequate training, will enable almost any composer so to employ the incalculably rich resources of modern music that he may set forth a dramatic text with a semblance of color and veracity. In Mr. Herbert's case it must not be forgotten that he was dealing in 'Natoma' with hopeless dramatic material; yet it is also true that had he been intended by the gods for a composer of serious music, an authentic power of eloquent and individual expression would have enabled him to triumph even over Mr. Redding's libretto—to seek out the reality of sentiment and passion and tragedy behind the frail and tottering structure of the dramatist and utter it with strength, with beauty, with distinction."

That criticism, however, was not altogether fair. There was then a terrific prejudice against American opera—based to some extent on previous unhappy experiences—and all musicians of discrimination went to hear a new American opera with their minds made up as to the outcome and sharply attuned to find the slightest flaw.

"Natoma" contains some very fine music. The fatalistic "Habanera" will live among the classic melodies; the "Dagger Dance" will be played by orchestras of the world as an example of American music; the "Boat Song" will be recognized as possessing an individual beauty meriting survival. The greatest fault of "Natoma" is its lack of unity. It is part comic and part serious opera; and the serious is very much so, expressed with a modernity of manner that makes the other portions stand out in emphatic contrast.

Herbert, a born sentimental melodist, tried to subordinate himself to the current conception of a grand opera composer. His original theory was, that since he was known as a composer of popular melodies, he should have no popular melodies at all in "Natoma"; he should confine himself to a Wagnerian-Straussian melodramatic speech. Then he was afraid that if he did so the opera might not be a success. He knew from experience that it was the melodies in a musical work that brought down the house. So he decided a compromise was the best plan—half light, half serious.

The critics' handling of Herbert was tender compared with the lambasting poor Redding received. They were merciless. But though the lyrics of "Natoma" are impossible and the dialogue poor, the plot is not bad for opera. The synopsis of the story is quite interesting.

The only critic who saw this favorable point was Henry T. Finck, and it inspired him to deliver one of the cleverest speeches, for a musician, on record.

It was made at a banquet tendered Victor Herbert and Redding by the New York Bohemian Club, at

Louis Martin's restaurant, in honor of the production of his opera. Dozens of men notable in the musical world were there. When Finck was called upon for an address he arose readily.

"Gentlemen," he said, "critics have a way of assailing librettos, but never have I seen so violent an onslaught as that made on a cetrain opera book I have in mind."

Some of the guests lowered their eyes and became intent on playing with their glasses. Redding turned red. Herbert looked blank. The eyes of Rubin Goldmark, the toastmaster, began to flash.

But Finck blandly ignored all the signs. He took up a sheaf of notes and calmly continued to speak.

"I have here some clippings of what five of the best known critics said about it. I will read a few: 'It is the most unfortunate choice of a book ever made by a really prominent composer!'—'The first act is intolerably tedious,'—'The love duo reveals a hopelessly poetic impotence,'—'Considered purely as a poem, few will be able to read it without comic emotions,'—'It is in every respect absurd.' "

There was silence in the room. Redding was gazing stonily into space. Unperturbed, Finck went on:

"Now, gentlemen, I know that Mr. Redding is right here. I have not yet had the pleasure of meeting him. But what's the difference anyway? The criticisms I have just read were not written about 'Natoma'; they were written about Richard Wagner's greatest music drama, 'Tristan and Isolde.' "

What applause for the wily Finck! And what a transition from hell to heaven for Redding!

When calm once more settled over the dining-room in Louis Martin's restaurant, Finck went on with some reminiscences of the composer:

"I have known Mr. Herbert for nearly a quarter of a century. From the beginning I praised his operettas —sometimes so warmly that letters were written to the *Evening Post* (Finck's paper) hinting at bribery. Bribery indeed! Why, gentlemen, I am actually seven dollars out of pocket because of my long friendship with Victor Herbert! You know that he lived and played for a long time in Stuttgart. Now when I first came to New York, I used to get my music sent over from Stuttgart by Zumsteeg. Zumsteeg was the publisher of Herbert's violoncello concerto, and, knowing that I played that instrument, and was a friend of Herbert's, he sent me a copy, followed by a bill for seven dollars. The concerto was too hard for me to play, but I kept it and got a money order for seven dollars. Don't you think, gentlemen, that about the meanest way a composer can raise money is by getting it out of a critic who praises him?

"Afterwards, when I heard him play that concerto at a Philharmonic concert I forgave him. Dvorák was present on that occasion, and was so pleased with the work that he praised it publicly."

The unusual spectacle of a passage at arms between a guest of honor and one of the other guests was seen at this banquet. Walter Damrosch had evoked memories of the *Courier* libel suit by praising Herbert for the fight he made against that journal—thereby showing the bias that doubtless actuated him at the trial. He painted an attractive picture of Herbert's future musical career. Krehbiel followed him and told a number of stories of Herbert's beginnings in New York. He told how he was introduced to Herbert in a restaurant by Anton Seidl, and, after acknowledging the introduction in German, he was surprised to hear Herbert speak English. In reply to his comment, Herbert had spoken up testily: "Well, why shouldn't I speak English? I'm an Irishman."

Herbert spoke after Krehbiel. He thanked those who had praised his work, and then unconventionally launched into a sharp attack on critics. He accused them of being hasty in their judgment, and unjust. He singled out his old friend, Krehbiel, and practically called him a liar for having stated in the *New York Tribune* that the audience at the second performance of "Natoma" at the Metropolitan had been small. Herbert declared the house had been sold out.

The toastmaster hastily arose and quashed the acrimonious discussion.

After the banquet, Herbert issued a statement to *Musical America* in explanation of his conduct:

"I did not mean to attack critics in my speech, but only intended to make an appeal for fair play. Good criticism is courted by the composer and musician. It is necessary; but in his review, the critic should tell what happened, and not pick to pieces one or two sections in an opera which displeased him. He should take into account the hard work that has been done by the composer and the librettist. I worked for sixteen hours a day on 'Natoma,' and have almost ruined my eyesight. I do not want flattery nor honeyed words. Many critics are men of splendid education and can point out defects in a score of which the composer never thought. But this should be done kindly.

"I do not believe that a person can write a fair review of a serious opera, such as 'Natoma,' after hearing it but once. And knowing this, see how absurd it is to write a review when one has heard only a snatch of a work, here or there, leaving, for instance, before the last act." (He was referring to certain critics he had watched zealously on the first night.)

Mary Garden sent a message to the banquet phrased in her own flamboyant style:

"All hail, Victor Herbert, the first writer of American grand opera! May it be the beginning of this great art which America does not yet hold! It is not America's fault—great, energetic country! But man's. They are too busy giving their brains to the making of this new world; giving its turn to be the glory of the universe, and grand opera would naturally be the last thought!

"So lift up your glass to its glory in the next century!
                                        "MARY GARDEN."

In spite of all that has been said about it, "Natoma" continues to be the most successful American grand opera. It had thirty-eight performances, far and away the record. Of course it must be taken into account that the Chicago Opera Company did much touring, and that each city they visited was anxious to hear the Herbert work. But it is also a fact that the audiences liked it. When it was presented in Chicago—with a slightly altered cast—the audience was most enthusiastic.

The Chicago Opera Company gave thirty performances altogether. Herbert himself conducted the last presentation. But it was without Mary Garden, for she had left the cast and her rôle was sung by Alice Zepilli. The other eight performances were given when Milton and Sargent Aborn revived the opera for a week at the Century Opera House, in New York, beginning April 13, 1914.

It is interesting to record here that when Mary Garden saw herself in the mirror as the Indian girl, "Natoma," she was abruptly awakened to the fact that she looked the hundred and sixty-nine pounds she weighed. After the season was over, she went on a diet and took a course of exercises. She lost thirty pounds by sweating at a rowing machine, drinking lemon water and substituting for a heavier supper the tails of six crawfishes.

XVII

At the same time that rehearsals for "Natoma" were in progress, Herbert was rehearsing a new operetta, "When Sweet Sixteen." The duality of the man again stands out here. The production of his first grand opera was going forward—the most important work of his career. It was a work in the category of the "serious" music to which he so aspired. And yet he could easily turn from it to a minor operetta.

"When Sweet Sixteen" was originally a play written by George V. Hobart for Grace George. Before it was quite finished, Miss George was chosen for the cast of the New Theater, the subsidized venture that was intended to be a home for pure drama and developed into a discouraging failure. Miss George was flattered by the distinction, and cast "When Sweet Sixteen" aside.

Hobart was most disappointed, for he saw no prospect of getting his play produced that season. He met Herbert and told him his trouble. Herbert thought that the play might make a good operetta, and promised, if Hobart made the necessary changes, to have it produced before the season was over.

Hobart agreed, and in two weeks the new version and the music were ready. Herbert found a manager who pledged himself to produce it within six weeks. The composer then went back to his "Natoma" rehearsals, and also to the rehearsals for "Naughty Marietta."

After some weeks passed, he discovered that "When Sweet Sixteen" had not been touched. He was forced by his promise to Hobart to begin hunting for another producer, and could find one only by pledging himself to conduct the orchestra in every city in which the piece should play during its preliminary tour.

Casting for "When Sweet Sixteen" began the next day. Rehearsals were conducted under Herbert's supervision for three weeks, and then the operetta went on the road. Altogether, Herbert traveled twelve thousand miles in commuting between opening nights and New York.

Herbert was moving at full speed at this time. He is described in the midst of his extraordinary activities by *Musical America:*

" 'His Sweet Sixteen' had its première in Toronto last week and will no doubt be coming to New York soon. . . . If happiness lies in keeping occupied, then there is probably no happier man in New York than Victor Herbert. His daily schedule runs about like this: At 1:30 A.M. he returns from Philadelphia, where he has rehearsed 'Natoma.' At 7 he gets up to meet a phonograph engagement that lasts three hours. At 10:30 he sees a reporter. From 12 until 3, he is correcting the proofs sent over from the printers (of 'Natoma'). From 3 to 4, another interview. At 4, the young woman cast for the leading rôle of a new comic opera arrives to run over her part with the composer.

From 5 to 7, he is working on another opera recently ordered to be completed in a stated number of days. At 8:15, he conducts a special performance of 'Naughty Marietta.' Then the midnight train again to Philadelphia.

"A week or two ago, Mr. Herbert was reminded of a promise he had made to write another operetta for Fritzi Scheff, and now, among other things, this is in preparation. It will probably be called 'Rosita.'"

What a madhouse life! Why Herbert should have piled up orders so is not easy to understand. He did not need money, though he spent much. He had every opportunity to take his work more leisurely and permit himself that ease for which artists who are hard-pressed financially and must keep up with the grind, pray. One explanation is that he had tremendous faith in his capacity for work and gloried in the volume of his output as other men glory in the strength of their muscles. It probably counterbalanced his disappointment at not being accepted as an important "serious" composer.

He was so driven for time that when he was composing "When Sweet Sixteen," he interpolated a good deal of the music from about half a dozen of his old operettas in the form of a medley.

On August 14, 1911, Herbert remembered the twenty-fifth anniversary of his marriage, and celebrated it by a large reception and garden party at his summer home at Lake Placid. About two hundred guests were present.

At the same time he received the degree of Doctor of Music from Villa Nova College, a Catholic institution in Pennsylvania. That degree brought him quite a bit of satiric comment.

"Naughty Marietta" marked the climax of Herbert's operetta career—as "Natoma" brought him up to his highest level as a composer of serious music. From then on his was a downward path.

Only two operettas gained a fair measure of success —"The Enchantress," written for Kitty Gordon, and "Princess Pat." H. T. Parker wrote a review of the former which should be included in the Herbert record because of the estimate of the composer's music by a keen, critical mind, and because it is a good description of Herbert's conducting. It was published in the *Boston Transcript*, November 12, 1912, and follows in part:

"At the end of the first act of 'The Enchantress,' midway in the first performance of the operetta in Boston at the Colonial last evening, the audience applauded heartily. When the answering curtain rose, Miss Kitty Gordon, the star of the piece, came promptly to the footlights and by word and gesture bade Victor Herbert, who was conducting his own music, join her on the stage. Thereupon the audience doubled and redoubled its clapping and would not still it until Mr. Herbert had made a homely little speech of thanks and sat down suddenly, in the course of a backward bow, upon the steps of the Balkan throne-room in which he was nominally standing. He turned the contretemps with an Irish smile and the spectators smiled amusedly back at him. Throughout the evening they were highly and justly pleased with his share of the entertainment. He cor ducted scarcely as any one else, unless it is Mr. de Novellis, conducts an operetta nowadays—kept and brightened the rhythm of each number, gave each quip of instrumental humor its true turn, carefully adjusted voices and orchestra, clothed every song with a musical individuality and stimulated the players on the stage and the bandsmen in the pit until both were on their mettle.

"Mr. Herbert has become a composer with more commissions than he can fulfill. He is writing, if report is true, another serious opera. These are large tasks; but if he would condescend once more to the conducting of operetta he would be worth his weight (which is considerable) in gold to the fortunate piece, manager and public. Unfortunately, the job is monotonous, and wisely Mr. Herbert chooses to make it, as he did last evening, an occasional pastime.

"The music of Mr. Herbert, the composer, deserved the pains of Mr. Herbert, the conductor, because, as he does not always do, when he is overcrowded with commissions, he had taken pains in the writing of it. He writes out of a store of musical learning and practice that the journeymen of Broadway would call erudition—did they know the word. Yet he uses his learning lightly and entertainingly, as when the song about happiness runs serio-comically into a sort of solemn ecclesiastical finale, or when he fills a pretty madrigal for five women's voices with many a quaint modulation or seemingly simple artifice. Out of the same knowledge and skill he can build up a chorus in a fashion that writers of choral music might envy, and that, piling sonority upon sonority, quite thrills the audience for operetta.

"Knowing the individual quality of an orchestra and having a lively fancy he is adept in little quips of instrumental humor, knowing the orchestra en masse and having a lively sense of an average audience he lets these quips 'through' so that they tell—quite as much, by the way, as did most of the spoken humors of 'The Enchantress.'

"Mr. Herbert has, besides, a happy and discriminating versatility. When he writes patter he makes it rhythmic and pointed. If he must turn a soubrette jingle, as he has twice to do in 'The Enchantress,' he makes it gay and saves it from cheapness. He writes his sentimental tunes with warm instrumental voices, yet almost always the melody runs rich and clear. He can make music of light and playful fancy, like the song of the goldfish or the madrigal in this same 'Enchantress.' His marches sound as do Sousa's—but with music. At his best—and he sustains his best through much of his newest operetta—we Americans may justly match him against the more vaunted composers of Vienna. Unlike many of them, he has a distinct individuality and fancy, and he ranges widely in the matter and the manner of his music. Like them, however, he has a clear sense of theatrical effect and an instinctive and practiced understanding of the musical capabilities and responsiveness of audiences for operetta. The proof was in the applause that rewarded his music at every turn last evening. Mr. Herbert even suppressed encores; yet his audience did not rebel. Irish exuberance makes his music bubble, while Irish humor and fancy spice it."

In 1914, another grand opera by Herbert was presented to a public still waiting to hear the great American opera. This was "Madeleine," produced at the Metropolitan Opera House, on January 24, 1914. The cast was composed of Frances Alda, in the rôle of "Madeleine," Leonora Sparkes, Pini-Corsi, and Althouse. Giorgio Polacco conducted. It was in one act, the libretto, by Grant Stewart, being derived from a French play by Decourelles and Thibaut which Herbert liked.

"Madeleine" was a failure.

When the critics, in reviewing "Natoma," referred to comic opera, Herbert had been nettled. In undertaking "Madeleine" he said to his friends: "Now I'll give them something they won't understand!"

So he wrote an opera without any melody, composed entirely of descriptive orchestration and melodic speech, an idiom completely foreign to him. The result was lamentable. There is only one fine passage in the entire act—a melody of only nine bars which comes at the end of "Madeleine's" aria, "A Perfect Day." For the rest, the piece is a bore. It is now as dead as the most obscure of Herbert's works.

[236]

At the same time Herbert had a comic opera, "The Debutante," on Broadway. It was playing at the Knickerbocker, right opposite the Metropolitan. This, too, was a failure, and Herbert was much depressed.

"The Debutante" was produced by John Fisher, the man who presented "Florodora." Matters had not been going well with Fisher and he had sunk all his remaining funds in the Herbert piece in a last effort to recoup. He lost about eighty thousand dollars on "The Debutante," and it broke his pocket and his heart. He had to take a job, brooded about it, and died.

During the run of this production Herbert lost much of his exuberant spirits. He used to come into the Knickerbocker every evening, sit down on the balcony steps with Harry Somers, the manager of the theater, and talk moodily or muse about old times. In his long association with Victor Herbert, Somers had never seen him so dispirited.

Perhaps the composer sensed the change that was soon to come to Broadway musical productions. Jazz had appeared. The first bands with their muted instruments were giving out barbaric sounds. In a few years the war was to bring an excited restlessness, a reaction against old forms which was to affect the stage greatly.

Dancing became the vogue among all classes—dancing at home, in restaurants, in dance halls; dancing to jazz rhythms began to dominate the stage.

The old operetta, with its reliance on romantic story, choral singing, ballads and substantial orchestral accompaniment was crowded out by an incoming horde of revues, and musical comedies in revue style.

Herbert had no relation with these productions. A new generation of song writers came in, men utterly conscienceless about music, knowing nothing of music as an art form, and caring nothing for it; men who, in most cases, could not even put down on paper what was published under their names—who wrote for the moment, not songs, but "numbers," without the least concern about the permanence of their work. With such men, too, Herbert had no relation.

Producers tried to interpolate jazz pieces into his scores but he fiercely repulsed them. He became rather a lonely figure, although his friendships were as numerous as ever, and his manner as jovial.

It was at about this time that a new interest came into his life: political Irish patriotism. The war began to segregate mankind into factions and Victor Herbert, the grandson of Samuel Lover, began to show himself increasingly to the public as the Irishman. That England was fighting Germany was sufficient to make him an ally of Germany; that he had lived so long in Germany and so well absorbed her culture, was a still greater reason to make him an enemy of England.

Yet it is to be doubted if he really was as bitter towards England as he sounded. His was an emotional, naïve antagonism; a legacy. There was not much thought or calculation about it. He was swayed, first by his family, and later by the American-Irishmen with whom he had come in contact when he first reached this country, and who had given him their respect and admiration because he was the offspring of a distinguished compatriot as well as for his own talents and his amiable personality. Had circumstances brought him into closer touch with England it is quite possible that his anti-English views would have been considerably modified.

As it was he never lost an opportunity to show what he thought of John Bull.

Among the most memorable of his activities in this direction was one that remained unknown to all but a few intimates. In 1914, Gene Buck was supervising the staging of the current edition of the Ziegfeld Follies. In view of the world situation, he thought it would be a good idea to have a finale called "The Parade of the Nations." He would have a number of the Ziegfeld beauties marching down the stage in the glorified manner, each representing a nation and each accompanied by that nation's anthem.

Having a great admiration for Herbert as a composer of ensembles and knowing his great skill as an orchestrater, Buck commissioned him to arrange the music.

The score for the "Parade" was finished the day before the opening of the Follies. As he handed him the manuscript, Herbert said:

"Gene, pay attention to this number."

"Why?" Buck asked.

"Oh, I've put a little joke into it. See if you can detect it."

When the time came, Buck did pay attention, but nothing happened. Then the orchestra played a rousing orchestration of "Die Wacht am Rhein," and a stately show girl proudly marched in as "Germany." She was followed by Justine Johnson, a noted beauty of her day, as "Britannia."

At this moment the orchestra became abruptly silent and from the void came forth "God Save the King," in a suggestive squeak from a single piccolo. The audience, even if somewhat puzzled, probably thought Herbert did this for contrast, especially as a crashing rendition of "The Star-Spangled Banner" followed the English anthem.

But Buck knew just what effect Herbert had planned.

Strangely enough, Herbert and his family had visited England in the earlier part of that year. He proclaimed himself a Home-Ruler but strenuously set about seeing all the sights of London. He visited the places where his grandfather had lived, and all the points of interest.

McKenzie Regan, the bandmaster of the famous Coldstream Guards, considered him a notable guest and entertained him royally. Regan had his band play a program at the Duke of York's school in Chelsea, and then showed him through Buckingham Palace.

But this was more than Herbert's Irish constitution could stand. He became ill inside the palace gates. Rather unsuitably for the ending to this story, it was found that he was not suffering from distress of mind, but had a prosaic attack of appendicitis.

The composer was always a member of Irish organizations and constantly attended their affairs. With Father Francis P. Duffy, he founded the Irish Musical Society. He organized the Glee Club of the Friendly Sons of St. Patrick, for whom he arranged many Irish folk songs. He was a member of that association and also of the Friends of Irish Freedom. In 1914, he was elected president of the former organization, and two years later he was president of the Friends.

His elevation to this office took place at the Irish Race Convention, March 4, 1916, in the Astor Hotel ballroom. It was a gathering which burned with Irish patriotic fervor and good will for Germany. The republicans believed that if Germany won the war it would release Ireland from English rule. One of the speakers, Jeremiah O'Leary, was so acutely pro-German that he insisted that all good Irishmen stand up when "Die Wacht am Rhein" was played. So ardent was the Hibernian spirit that a priest apologized for his English accent.

A report of this gathering in the *Gaelic American* gives a picture of Herbert that is in strange contrast to the Herbert so popular on Broadway:

"When Victor Herbert, the great composer and president of the Friendly Sons of St. Patrick, stepped to the platform to call the convention to order, the scene was the most inspiring one that ever greeted the eyes of Irish men and women in America. The throng of men and women that filled every available seat, crowded the galleries and stood in aisles, had been

whiling away the time chatting and exchanging greet-
ings. When Mr. Herbert's gavel rapped for order,
every man and woman stood up and gave such a wild
Irish cheer as had never echoed in any New York
meeting hall before and it was some moments before
his voice could be heard. He looked supremely happy
that the distinction of calling the Convention to order
had been assigned him and at the enthusiastic welcome
accorded him. When the great audience sat down, he
announced Justice W. Goff as temporary Chairman and
appointed a committee to escort him to the chair. Then
the audience sprang to its feet again and another trio
of vigorous Irish cheers shook the building."

In becoming the head of the important Friends of
Irish Freedom, Herbert became one of the leaders of
American-Irish patriotism—not because of any quali-
ties of leadership, but because of his name and prestige.
His duties in connection with the societies over which
he presided were rather perfunctory. He was entirely
influenced by his associates in the movement. He was
vigorously against the League of Nations because his
friend, Judge Daniel F. Cohalan, was against it. Judge
Cohalan was one of his mentors and helped him considerably with any speeches or statements his official
position obliged him to make.

A few weeks after his election to the presidency of
the Friends of Irish Freedom, there was presented the
rare spectacle of Victor Herbert as an erudite author.
He wrote a long political article for the *New York*

Sun, in answer to Sir Edward Carson and John Redmond, whose statements had previously been published in the same newspaper. The article begins:

"If England could win the war by diplomacy or by some means other than fighting, there would be no doubt of the outcome of the conflict, but unfortunately for her, and very fortunately for what I believe to be the best interests of mankind in general, and of Ireland in particular, she is now fighting against foes whom she cannot frighten nor cajole, and in my judgment, from the outbreak of the war, it has seemed inevitable that the British Empire is doomed, and that again we are going to live in a world where there will be liberty and freedom, and where the weaker people will not have to live in constant dread that their countries and their rights are to be taken away from them. Such a result will bring happiness to many lands, but to none other in such measure as to the land of my birth. . . ."

And towards the end of the article:

"In spite of the sophistry of Carson and the *raimeis* of Redmond, the Irish at home and abroad, with their old instinct as a fighting race, recognize and feel that England is being beaten in this present war. They have no sympathy or pity for the country which has ever tyrannized over the weak and truckled to the strong. Ireland to-day, Mr. Redmond to the contrary notwithstanding, is not with England, and every day is preparing more and more to look out for herself."

The article bristles with historical facts, statesmanlike comments, and oratorical exhortations. All from the genial Victor! The Victor whose most familiar pronouncement was a booming laugh, quickly drowned in a cascade of beer!

Of course, only a small part, if any part at all, of this statement was written by Herbert. It was prepared by Judge Cohalan. But it bore the signature of Victor Herbert, and was thus broadcast throughout the world.

After this it often was, "Herbert Refutes Figures," "Herbert Gives the Lie to Carson," etc. He was called upon to be present at many Irish meetings, but his duties were over when he had introduced the chairman for the occasion. Poor Herbert, although extremely proud of his new political distinction, was much more at home at a Lambs Club Gambol.

Judge Cohalan relates that Herbert was rather subdued when in the presence of the Irish intellectuals over whom he was leader. There often were gatherings of such groups, which included men like Judge Goff, Judge O'Gorman, John J. Delaney, Joseph I. C. Clark, Judge John Jerome, a gentleman named Rooney, who was in the Corporation Counsel's office and wrote the lyrics for some of Herbert's songs, and others noted in the New York Irish community. Occasionally Herbert would hold his own in the conversations, but by these friends, he was regarded as having a slower mind.

In October, 1916, the Irish and German societies of New York united in sponsoring a bazaar for the benefit of the Irish Relief Fund at Madison Square Garden.

Herbert had a carefully prepared address for the occasion, and led off by reading: "I rejoice in seeing this great crowd before me—" In the confusion of his speech-making, he forgot that there were only about fifteen hundred people of each nationality present—a slight number in the vastness of the Garden.

At the Actors' Fund Fair in Grand Central Palace the following year, he was leading the grand march when he noticed a pig in an Irish booth. He grabbed the animal, tied a green ribbon around its neck, dubbed it "Victor," and delightedly led it around the hall all night.

He was good entertainment at Irish gatherings and had a favorite story which is remembered by his friends. This concerned General Phil Sheridan, who is claimed by the Irish. Sheridan was military commander of Texas during the Civil War, said Herbert, and the people there made it unpleasant for him. He was happy when released and returned to Washington, where he saw Grant.

"How do you like Texas?" asked the general.

"Well," replied Sheridan, "if I owned two houses, one in hell and one in Texas, I'd live in the house in hell and rent the one in Texas."

As an example of Herbert's aversion to England, Henry K. Hadley relates that when he returned from an engagement in that country, Herbert asked him:

"Well, how did you find the orchestras there?" But before Hadley could reply, Herbert cut him off with: "I bet you found few good snare-drummers—I know

—you don't have to tell me!   I know they were lousy!"

But his fealty to everything that was even distantly related to Ireland showed itself when, in 1924, he was one of a committee of song writers who went to Washington to fight against the free use of music by radio stations.   The committee had just been introduced to President Coolidge and shaken his hand, one by one. Charles K. Harris was behind Herbert, and just as they were walking out after the ceremony Herbert remarked to Harris in a low voice:

"I'm going to vote for Al Smith just the same."

XVIII

As his operettas grew weaker in their drawing power, Herbert took to writing special numbers for revues. He would work for the new forms of Broadway productions, but he intended to do only such numbers as suited him.

He proved quite adept. Ned Wayburn tells of his expertness in writing music to fit certain dancing scenes —never jazz, of course. When Wayburn was staging "Miss 1917," at the Century, he designed an "Uncle Sam" finale. In this scene sailor boys and girls were to march on a special imposed stage in opposite formation. Wayburn commissioned Herbert to do the music. The composer came down to a rehearsal and Wayburn put his people through the dance number. There was no music of any sort, the chorus merely doing the kind of tap dance Wayburn wanted.

Herbert had taken off his coat and sat down before the piano. He watched and listened. Then he wrote a translation of the tap dance in the form of a drum part. (The notation for drums is merely a series of rhythm indications.)

"I'll have it ready for you to-morrow at this time," he told Wayburn.

Sharp at two the next afternoon, the same hour Herbert had left the rehearsal the day before, he delivered the composition. Wayburn was delighted with it. It was just the music he had imagined for such a scene.

But the Herbert popularity was fading; he was becoming a figure from a past day. He had placed much hope in a new piece, "Orange Blossoms." It failed, and his intimates saw how badly he felt. For the first time he appeared worried. People used to ask him why he didn't write another "Kiss Me Again" waltz, and he would sadly reply that he had written waltzes as good, but that the public had changed. It did not recognize them.

He was right to a large extent. He still wrote music which equaled his earlier work. There was a song which Ned Wayburn liked in "Orange Blossoms." When he staged the Ziegfeld "Follies of 1923," he asked permission to interpolate it in the Follies. That was "A Kiss in the Dark," one of Herbert's most popular songs.

In that same year—1923—he was engaged to write overtures and conduct the orchestra at the Cosmopolitan Theater, at Columbus Circle, where a series of Marion Davies pictures were to be shown. He wrote overtures for several pictures, among them, "Little Old New York," "Under the Red Robe," and "Yolanda," but his name failed to attract audiences, as had been hoped, and the venture was a failure. He was paid sixty thousand dollars for his year's contract, but the picture people decided it was cheaper to pay Herbert his salary than to incur the expense of the orchestra. So his men were dismissed, and Herbert put in an appearance at the theater every Saturday to draw his check and to make the formal statement: "If you want me, I'm here."

Wayburn had intended that Herbert should write the music for the 1923 Follies, but it was finally decided to get some more modern composer. Herbert was to be used only to compose the finale of the second act. For some reason, the production plans were changed and the date for the opening advanced. According to Wayburn, the show was not ready, and when eight carloads of scenery—to be hung and set for the first time —were dumped backstage on the afternoon before the opening night, Wayburn was desperate. At two o'clock, Herbert strolled in.

"He tore his hair," said Wayburn, "when he saw what was going on. 'You can't do it!' he cried. 'It's suicide!' I told him we had to go through with it, and he asked me when he should come that night to conduct the finale. I told him I had no idea.

Herbert came back at eight o'clock, dressed in his best, and waited to be called into the orchestra pit. He waited, and waited, and waited. Eleven o'clock came, the ordinary closing time for theaters, and still the show lumbered on; twelve o'clock, and no end in sight.

Ordinarily, Herbert would have gone home in disgust; but it was not often now that he conducted a show. So he waited. It was hot and stuffy in the dressing-room. Herbert suffered great discomfort from heat and always tore off his clothes. But he didn't dare this time; at any minute he might be called out. So he sat and waited. One o'clock, and still no call. Wilted, suffering, dazed, he could not bring himself to leave without conducting the finale. Two o'clock found him still waiting. At last, at five minutes after two, the call came. Herbert rose wearily and walked into the pit.

Many of the audience had gone home. Those who remained were tired and anxious to leave. And it was for this depressing house that Herbert conducted his finale—his last appearance as a conductor in a theater.

He had one more spurt of celebrity. Radio had come into the world. It cut the composers' incomes, because people heard the new songs over the air, and so found no need to buy records, sheet music or piano rolls. As usual, Herbert was in the forefront in the ensuing fight for composers' rights. He went with a delegation of his colleagues to Washington and was active in the arguments before the legislative committee. He was the old Herbert there, happy in being surrounded by so many of his friends. He insisted on treating every one at the Willard Hotel, and sang and played the cello for the newspaper men.

In 1924 he was engaged to write numbers for the new Ziegfeld Follies. A retainer of a hundred and fifty dollars a week was paid him.

On Monday morning, May 27, 1924, Herbert was conferring with Florenz Ziegfeld in the latter's office. Both men had been up late the night before, rehearsing the music already written.

At twelve o'clock, Herbert left for luncheon at the

Lambs Club, promising Ziegfeld to be back that afternoon at two-thirty. At the club Charles K. Harris was
sitting at a table before a plate of wheatcakes and just
as he was about to cut into them he felt an arm about
his shoulders. He looked up to see the smiling face of
Victor Herbert.

"Don't eat those—they aren't good for you," Herbert admonished.

"What's the difference," objected Harris, "so long
as they agree with me?"

"Charley," Herbert declared, "you and I are getting too old for wheatcakes."

They both laughed, then suddenly Harris became
serious.

"I have some bad news for you, Victor," he said.

Those words were the usual preface to the announce-
ment that a club member had died and that they were
to attend the funeral.

"Who is it to-day?" Herbert asked.

"Teddy Morse," Harris replied.

Morse was a song writer who had some popular compositions to his credit—"Goodbye, Dolly Gray," among
them.

Herbert was shocked and walked silently away to join
some friends at another table. A little later, Harris,
seeing Herbert about to bite into a sandwich, walked
over to his table and put his arm about Herbert's
shoulders.

"Victor," he said, laughing, "take my advice and
don't eat a sandwich. It will give you indigestion."

"Charley," vowed Herbert, "I can eat nails."

The composer finished his lunch, left the club-house, and was about to return to the Ziegfeld office when he suddenly felt ill. He decided to go to his home, at 300 W. One-Hundred-and-Eighth Street. But he felt no better there.

Then he telephoned his physician, Dr. Emanuel Baruch, at 57 East Seventy-seventh Street, that he was coming to see him. He got into his car and drove over.

In the meantime, Dr. Baruch had been called away for a consultation. When Herbert arrived, he was informed that the doctor would be in shortly. He went out to the front of the private stone house and chatted pleasantly with an acquaintance. Suddenly he collapsed.

It was at that moment that Dr. Baruch returned. Herbert was carried into the office and all possible restoratives applied, but without success. Victor Herbert was dead.

"He would not have lived, even if I had come earlier," said Dr. Baruch. "His body had reached its limit, and just gave out."

The official diagnosis was heart failure.

Broadway was literally stunned when it heard the news. It could not believe that its Victor Herbert was no more. He had been so radiantly alive just a few hours before! So many people had seen him, with so many he had talked and joked, at so many he had smiled!

At the moment of his death, an orchestra over the radio station WEAF was playing a selection from his

"It Happened in Nordland." In the Ziegfeld office they were impatiently awaiting him. It seemed incomprehensible that Herbert should so suddenly vanish from the musical and theatrical life of America.

Henry K. Hadley was conducting the Worcester Festival at the time. That night he received a message from the manager of Herbert's orchestra. He returned to New York the next morning, and the following morning went to Carnegie Hall, where the Herbert orchestra was to have had a rehearsal with their conductor in preparation for the Willow Grove Park summer concerts. The men were all there, sad, bewildered, forlorn, their hands heavy on their instruments.

Hadley told them he was to conduct the Willow Grove concerts. He had previously given instructions to the librarian to lay out the gayest piece of Herbert's music he could find. The librarian selected an excerpt from the "Little Old New York" overture. Over it, on the stands, lay the trio from Chopin's funeral march.

Hadley raised his baton. The most poignant melody ever written trembled over the orchestra. When the soft, concluding note was played, the note of promise, like an apotheosis, the music paused. Then it burst into the joyous measures of the melody that pictured the bright New York that Herbert had loved so well. The sorrow was relieved. But two hours later, the men marched behind the casket of their late master.

The melancholy rites of the funeral were held on Wednesday, May 29, 1924, at one o'clock. At ten o'clock, Herbert's friends had attended the funeral of Teddy Morse.

The Herbert funeral procession formed at the clubhouse of the American Society of Authors, Composers and Publishers, at 56 West Forty-fifth street. Traffic was stopped on Fifth Avenue, the road of the march. The cortège was headed by the Police Band, playing the Chopin funeral march, and the hearse was flanked on each side by a squad of soldiers from Governor's Island, and by a company of Marines from the Brooklyn Navy Yard.

Behind, in a closed car, was the widow, silent, shrouded and bowed. At her side was her daughter, Ella. Then, in order, came members of the Lambs Club, the Friars, the Lotus Club, the Irish organizations, the Musicians' Union, and a detachment of the One-Hundred-and-Second Engineers, formerly the Twenty-second Regiment, whose band the dead man had helped make famous.

The service was conducted at St. Thomas Episcopal Church by the Rev. Dr. Ernest M. Stires. Anna Fitzui, the opera soprano, sang "Lead Kindly Light," and Nathan Franko played Bach's "Air on the G String."

The church was thronged with celebrities, but among those who came to pay tribute to a loved public figure, was a little Italian hurdy-gurdy man. He brought a wooden box and stood on it silently as the flower-strewn casket was borne out.

The body was taken to Woodlawn Cemetery. The

soldiers fired a volley, a bugler sounded taps, and Victor Herbert was definitely gone from the world.

A month later, on June 10, the remains were transferred to a mausoleum, a structure of white granite and bronze doors, surrounded by evergreens and shrubbery.

Herbert's estate, valued at "over $30,000," was left to his family. He bequeathed only $10,000 to his son, stating in his will: "My reason for this distribution of the property is that my son has received a good education and has been the recipient of many benefactions during my life and should be able to provide for himself without any further assistance from me."

But when his wife died not long after, her estate amounted to $209,734, the bulk of it in securities and bonds. She gave a life interest in $150,000 to Clifford, and the balance to her daughter. If the children should die without issue this money will go for hospital beds in memory of Victor Herbert.

When Herbert's home was sold at auction after his death his collection of scores, books, antiques and manuscripts brought $25,000. The orchestra scores were purchased by the Roxy Theatre for the use of its orchestra.

An unfortunate squabble arose when a bronze bust of Herbert by Edmond Quinn, intended for a place on the Mall, in Central Park, near the bandstand, was rejected by the Municipal Art Commission because they considered the spot too important for the man. Later, the disagreement was smoothed over and the bust unveiled in Central Park on November 30, 1927. A replica of it is in the foyer of the Roxy Theatre.

In the statement by Herbert's publishers when the estate was being settled, these works were listed among his failures: "The Debutante," "The Madcap Duchess," "Sweethearts," "My Golden Girl," "The Girl in the Spotlight," "Orange Blossoms," "Angel Face," "Her Regiment," and "Oui Madame."

His last operetta, "My Dream Girl," was a partial success. The waltz song of the same title from that production is proof that the Herbert melodic vein had not been worked out. It is a lovely little piece, and it is surprising that it is so little played or sung.

For other reasons now, Herbert's works attained greater popularity than ever. The radio developed into a household necessity and the music of Victor Herbert became as staple as the classics. To fill their myriad programs, the studio directors had to ransack the musical literature of the world. In Herbert's music they found a large store of pretty, ingratiating, charming and beautifully orchestrated numbers. His was just the music to broadcast.

Then, too, came the production of "The Student Prince," with its introduction of male choruses and its emphasis on romantic music. It brought back a vogue for the operetta. Melodies of the old type again began to be heard in the land.

Thus the name of Victor Herbert has become one of the most familiar to issue from the loud speakers of millions of radios. His music is heard with fond memories by an older generation and with the delight of discovery by the younger.

Deems Taylor's remark that Victor Herbert never wrote a vulgar line has been taken up by the composer's friends as a sort of memorial slogan. That may or may not be true. It is doubtful whether any one has so thoroughly combed the great mass of music that Victor Herbert left that he is qualified to make such a statement. To the contrary, many of Herbert's operetta songs are quite commonplace. Victor Herbert's fame is not based on such a valueless claim as that he never wrote a vulgar line, but on the fact that he wrote many beautiful ones. He wrote songs and melodies that are beloved by a nation. Most of all, he was the best composer of light music that the United States has developed as well as one of that small group of world composers who have a permanent place in musical history as masters of the operetta.

APPENDIX

PUBLISHED COMPOSITIONS OF VICTOR HERBERT

This list includes only Herbert's original compositions and is exclusive of the numerous instrumental and vocal arrangements made of his works. The German songs were all written during his early years.

Publications of Herbert by Luckhardt, Berlin, have been taken over by Heinrichshofens Verlag, Magdeburg, Germany; the Simrock, Berlin, publications, by H. J. Benjamin, Leipzig; the Dieckmann, Leipzig, publications are handled by K. F. Koeler, book jobbers, of Leipzig, and Zumsteeg is still in Stuttgart.

Songs

Blumlein am Herzen: "Hast ein blaublumelein einst mir gegeben." Op. 4. German and English text. Published by Zumsteeg, Stuttgart.

Das Geheimniss: "Heckenroslein, uber nacht." Op. 14. German and English text. Published by Luckhardt, Berlin.

Die Stille Rose: "Wenn auf der Erde Schweigen." Op. 15. German and English text. Published by Dieckmann, Leipzig, and Edward Schuberth, New York.

Dir Schonheit Krone: "Mein Schatzelein froh sing ich dir." Op. 5. For male quartet. Published by Zumsteeg, Stuttgart.

Dream On (Indian Lullaby), lyric by B. G. DeSylva. Published by Harms, New York.

Du Ahnst es Nicht: "Mein blick ruht auf dir." Op. 15. For mezzo-soprano. German and English text. Published by Luckhardt, Berlin.

Equity Star. Lyric by Grant Stewart. Published by Harms, New York.

Farewell (Dream Song). Lyric by Edward Locke. Published by Harms, New York.

Fliege fort, du klein waldvogelein. Op. 18. German and English text. Published by Luckhardt, Berlin.

Frieden: "Es ragt das gold'ne saatensfeld." For alto. German and English text. Published by Dieckmann, Leipzig, and Edward Schuberth, New York.

Frülingslied: "Mit frühlingsglantz im bluthenschnee." Op. 14. German and English text. Published by Luckhardt, Berlin.

Gestandniss: "Als liebchen ich zuerst dich sah." Op. 13. German and English text. Also with orchestral accompaniment. Published by Luckhardt, Berlin.

Geweihte Statte: "Wo zweie sich kussen zum ersten mal." Op. 13. German and English text. Published by Luckhardt, Berlin.

God Spare the Emerald Isle. Lyric by William Jerome. Published by Harms, New York.

Heart of Mine. Lyric by Lawrence Eyre. Published by Harms, New York.

Heimweh: "Die heimat fern, mit nassem blick." For alto. German and English text. Published by Dieckmann, Leipzig, and Edward Schuberth, New York.

Ich Liebe Dich: "Wie so verwandelt fuhl ich mich." Op. 14. German and English text. Published by Luckhardt, Berlin.

If You Love But Me. Published by Witmark, New York.

Jenny's Baby. Published by Edward Schuberth, New York.

Liebesleben: "Könnt in ein wort ich legen." Op. 15. German and English text. Published by Dieckmann, Leipzig, and Edward Schuberth, New York.

Liebeslied: "Ohne flamme brennt kein licht." For alto. German and English text. Published by Dieckmann, Leipzig, and Edward Schuberth, New York.

Lora Lee. Lyric by Joseph J. C. Clarke. Published by Harms, New York.

Lovelight (Dream Song). Lyric by Edward Locke. Published by Harms, New York.

Love's Hour. Lyric by Rida Johnson Young. Written for and sung by Luisa Tetrazzini. Published by G. Schirmer, New York.

Mary, Come Over to Me. Lyric by Irving Caesar. Published by Harms, New York.

Mary's Lamb. Published by Edward Schuberth, New York.

Molly, An Irish Love Song. Lyric by Rida Johnson Young. Published by Witmark, New York.

Mein Herz ist treu: "Der liebsten namen schreib ich im sand." Op. 21. For mezzo-soprano. German and English text. Published by Luckhardt, Berlin.

Nur du Bist's: "Lass mich zum letztenmal dir sagen." Op. 15. German and English text. Published by Dieckmann, Leipzig, and Edward Schuberth, New York.

Old Ireland Shall Be Free. Four-Part Song. Published by Witmark, New York.

Remembrance. Lyric by Carl Weitbrecht. Published by G. Schirmer, New York.

Schnelle Bluthe: "Madchen ging im feld allein." Op. 18. For mezzo-soprano. German and English text. Published by Luckhardt, Berlin.

Standchen: "Traute laute, lass ertonen." Op. 14. German and English text. Also published with orchestral accompaniment. Published by Luckhardt, Berlin.

Sweet Harp of the Day. Published by Edward Schuberth, New York.

The Time Will Come: "Who dares ride abroad so fierce!" Published by Dieckmann, Leipzig.

Vogelfang: "Man fangt die vogel gross und klein." Op. 10. From "Lieder eines fahrenden Gesellen, von Baumbach." German and English text. Published by Luckhardt, Berlin.

When Knighthood Was in Flower. Lyric by William LeBaron. Published by Harms, New York.

APPENDIX

Wirthstochterlein: "Und warst du, traute ein Engelein." Op. 10. From: "Lieder eines fahrenden Gesellen, von Baumbach." Published by Luckhardt, Berlin.

Piano Compositions

Air de Ballet. Published by G. Schirmer, New York.
Al Fresco. Published by Witmark, New York.
American Best Composition, two volumes of selected piano music. Editor-in-chief, Victor Herbert. Associated editors: Fanny Morris Smith and Louis R. Dressler. Published (1900) by the University Society.
American Girl March. Published by Edward Schuberth, New York.
Badinage. Published by Edward Schuberth, New York.
Belle of Pittsburgh March. Published by Edward Schuberth, New York.
Devotion. Published by T. B. Harms, New York.
Eldorado March. Published by Edward Schuberth, New York.
Estellita, Waltz. Published by Witmark, New York.
Fleurette, Waltz. Published by Witmark, New York.
Ghazel, Improvization. Published by Witmark, New York.
Indian Summer. Published by T. B. Harms, New York.
La Coquette, Valse Brilliante. Published by Witmark, New York.
Marion Davies March. Published by T. B. Harms, New York.
Mountain Brook, Imitative. Published by Witmark, New York.
On the Promenade, Morceau. Published by Witmark, New York.
On Your Way. One-Step. Published by Witmark, New York.
Ocean Breezes. Published by Edward Schuberth, New York.
Pan Americana, Morceau characteristique. Published by Witmark, New York. (Later orchestrated by Otto Langey.)
President's March. Published by Luckhardt, Berlin.
Punchinello, Characteristic. Published by Witmark, New York.
Under the Elms, Souvenir de Saratoga. Published by Witmark, New York.
Valse a la Mode. Published by Witmark, New York.
Whispering Willows, Intermezzo. Published by Witmark, New York.
Yesterthoughts, Meditation. Published by Witmark, New York.

Violin Compositions with Piano Accompaniment

A La Valse. Published by G. Schirmer, New York.
Floretta. Published by Witmark, New York.
Little Red Lark, Old Irish. Published by Witmark, New York.
Mirage. Published by G. Schirmer, New York.
Pensee Amoureuse. Published by Ricordi, New York.
Petite Valse. Published by Ricordi, New York.
Romance. Published by Ricordi, New York.
Arrangement of the Intermezzo from "Cavalleria Rusticana." Published by Edward Schuberth, New York.

Cello Compositions, with Piano or Orchestral Accompaniment

Berceuse. Published by Witmark, New York.
Concerto, No. 2. Op. 30. Published by Edward Schuberth, New York.

APPENDIX

Pensee Amoureuse. Published by Ricordi, New York.
Petite Valse. Published by Ricordi, New York.
Romance. Published by Ricordi, New York.
Suite. Op. 3. Published by Zumsteeg, Stuttgart. In five movements: Allegro Moderato, Scherzo, Andante, * Serenade (Andantino grazioso), Tarantelle.
Arrangement of "La Cinquantaine," by Gabriel-Marie. Published by Edward Schuberth, New York.

Flute and Clarinet Duet

L'Encore. Published by Witmark, New York.

Compositions for Orchestra

Air de ballet. (For String Orchestra with harp and triangle.) Published by G. Schirmer, New York.
American Fantasy. Published by Dieckmann, Leipzig.
A Suite of Serenades. For Jazz Orchestra. Published by T. B. Harms, New York. In four movements: Spanish, Chinese, Cuban, Oriental.
Cannibal Dance. Published by Carl Fischer, New York.
Danse Baroque. Published by Carl Fischer, New York.
Devastation. Published by Carl Fischer, New York.
Entrance of the Heroes. Published by Carl Fischer, New York.
Forebodings. Published by Carl Fischer, New York.
Forget-me-not. Published by G. Schirmer, New York.
Gate City March. Published by Carl Fischer, New York.
Heart Throbs. Published by Carl Fischer, New York.
Hero and Leander. Suite. Published by G. Schirmer, New York.
Irish Rhapsody. Published by G. Schirmer, New York.
Karma. Dramatic Prelude. Published by Carl Fischer, New York.
Little Italy. Hurdy-gurdy characteristic, with hand organ. Published by Carl Fischer, New York.
Love Sonnet. Published by Carl Fischer, New York.
Mystic Rider. Dramatic Allegro. Published by Carl Fischer, New York.
Persian Dance. Published by Carl Fischer, New York.
Persian March. Published by Carl Fischer, New York.
Punch and Judy. Humorous. Published by Carl Fischer, New York.
Sunset. (For string orchestra.) Published by G. Schirmer, New York.
Serenade. For strings. Op. 12. Published by Luckhardt, Berlin.
Woodland Fancies. Suite. Published by G. Schirmer, New York. In four movements: Morning in the Mountains, Forest Sylphs, Twilight, Autumn Frolics.
Suite Romantique. Published by Simrock, Berlin. In four movements: Visions, Aubade, Triomphe d'Amour, Fete Nuptiale.
The Jester's Serenade. Published by Carl Fischer, New York.
The Knight's Tournament. Published by Carl Fischer, New York.
The Rabble. Published by Carl Fischer, New York.
Under the Red Robe. Selections from the motion picture score. Published by G. Schirmer, New York.

* This movement became popular in various transcriptions.

APPENDIX

Orchestral Arrangements

At Dawning, by Charles Wakefield Cadman. Published by Carl Fischer, New York.

Kamenoi Ostrow, by Anton Rubinstein. Published by G. Schirmer, New York.

Liebestraum, by Franz Liszt. Published by G. Schirmer, New York

Minute Waltz, by Franz Chopin. Published by G. Schirmer, New York.

Scarf Dance, by Cecile Chaminade. Published by G. Schirmer, New York.

The Cat and the Mice and the Donkey and Driver, by Leonard. Published by G. Schirmer, New York.

The Flatterer, by Cecile Chaminade. Published by G. Schirmer, New York.

Compositions for Band

Centennial March. Published by Carl Fischer, New York.

Eldorado March. Published by Carl Fischer, New York.

Inauguration March. Published by Carl Fischer, New York.

Twenty-second Regiment March. Published by Carl Fischer.

Choral Compositions

Columbia Anthem. Unison chorus with piano accompaniment, later arranged by Victor Herbert for orchestra and band accompaniment. Published by Schuberth, New York.

Call to Freedom. Patriotic Ode for solo and mixed voices. Text by Victor Herbert. Published (1918) by Oliver Ditson Co., Boston.

Christ Is Risen. Four-part anthem. Published by Witmark, New York.

Die Versunkene Stadt: "Fernher tonte Cicadensang." Op. 20. German and English text. For male chorus. Published by Luckhardt, Berlin.

The Cruiskeen Lawn. Old Irish Air. For men's voices, a cappella. Published by G. Schirmer, New York.

The Hail of the Friendly Sons. For men's voices, a cappella. Published by G. Schirmer, New York.

The New Ireland. For men's voices, a cappella. Published by G. Schirmer, New York.

The Sunken City. For men's voices. Published by G. Schirmer, New York.

Wenn im Purpurschein. Op. 20. From: "Lieder eines fahrenden Gesellen," text by von Baumbach. For male chorus. Published by Luckhardt, Berlin. With English and German text.

Cantata

The Captive. Op. 25. For solo voices, chorus and orchestra. Written for the Worcester, Mass., Festival, September, 1891. Text, in German, by Rudolph von Baumbach. With English translation. Published by Luckhardt, Berlin.

APPENDIX

Operas

Natoma. Libretto by Joseph D. Redding. In three acts. Published by G. Schirmer, New York.

Madeleine. Libretto adapted from the French of Decourcelles and Thibaut, by Grant Stewart. In one act. Published by G. Schirmer, New York.

Operettas
(In chronological order)

Prince Ananias. Libretto by Francis Neilsen. 1894. Published by Schuberth, New York.

Wizard of the Nile. Libretto by Harry B. Smith. 1895. Published by Schuberth, New York.

The Gold Bug. Libretto by Glen MacDonough. 1896. Published by Schuberth, New York.

The Idol's Eye. Libretto by Harry B. Smith. 1897. Published by Schuberth, New York.

The Serenade. Libretto by Harry B. Smith. 1897. Published by Schuberth and Carl Fischer, New York.

The Fortune Teller. Libretto by Harry B. Smith. 1898. Published by Witmark, New York.

The Singing Girl. Book by Stanislaus Stange; lyrics by Harry B. Smith. 1899. Published by Witmark, New York.

Cyrano De Bergerac. Libretto by Harry B. Smith. 1899. Published by Witmark, New York.

The Ameer. Libretto by Frederic Rancken and Kirke La Shelle. 1899. Published by Witmark, New York.

The Viceroy. Libretto by Harry B. Smith. 1900. Published by Witmark, New York.

Babette. Libretto by Harry B. Smith. 1903. Published by Witmark, New York.

Babes in Toyland. Libretto by Glen MacDonough. 1903. Published by Witmark, New York.

Mlle. Modiste. Libretto by Henry Blossom. 1905. Published by Witmark, New York.

It Happened in Nordland. Libretto by Glen MacDonough. 1905. Published by Witmark, New York.

Miss Dolly Dollars. Libretto by Harry B. Smith. 1905. Published by Witmark, New York.

Wonderland. Libretto by Glen MacDonough. 1905. Published by Witmark, New York.

The Red Mill. Libretto by Henry Blossom. 1906. Published by Witmark, New York.

Dream City and Magic Knight. Libretto by Edgar Smith. 1906. Published by Charles K. Harris, New York.

The Tattooed Man. Libretto by Harry B. Smith. 1907. Published by Witmark, New York.

The Prima Donna. Libretto by Henry Blossom. 1908. Published by Witmark, New York.

Little Nemo. Libretto by Harry B. Smith. 1908. Published by Cohan and Harris Publishing Co., New York.

Rose of Algeria. Libretto by Glen MacDonough. 1909. Published by Charles K. Harris, New York.

Old Dutch. Libretto by G. S. Hobart. 1909. Published by Witmark, New York.

Naughty Marietta. Libretto by Rida Johnson Young. 1910. Published by Witmark, New York.

When Sweet Sixteen. Libretto by G. S. Hobart. 1910. Published by Witmark, New York.

The Enchantress. Libretto by Harry B. Smith. 1911. Published by Witmark, New York.

The Lady of the Slipper. Libretto by Anne Caldwell, Lawrence McCarty and James O'Dea. 1912. Published by Witmark, New York.

The Madcap Duchess. Libretto by David Stevens and Justin McCarthy. 1913. Published by Schirmers, New York.

Sweethearts. Libretto by Harry B. Smith and Fred de Gressac; lyrics by Robert B. Smith. 1913. Published by G. Schirmer, New York.

Angel Face. Libretto by Harry B. Smith. 1913. Published by T. B. Harms, New York.

The Debutante. Libretto by Harry B. Smith; lyrics by Robt. B. Smith. 1914. Published by G. Schirmer, New York.

The Only Girl. Libretto by Henry Blossom. 1914. Published by Witmark, New York.

Princess Pat. Libretto by Henry Blossom. 1915. Published by Witmark, New York.

Eileen. Libretto by Henry Blossom. 1917. Published by Witmark, New York.

Her Regiment. Libretto by William LeBaron. 1917. Published by T. B. Harms, New York.

The Velvet Lady. Libretto by Henry Blossom. 1919. Published by Witmark.

My Golden Girl. Libretto by Frederic Arnold Kummer. 1919. Published by T. B. Harms, New York.

The Girl in the Spotlight. Book by Harry B. Smith; lyrics by Robert B. Smith. 1920. Published by T. B. Harms, New York.

Oui, Madame. Book and lyrics by G. M. Wright and Robert B. Smith. 1920. Published by T. B. Harms, New York.

Orange Blossoms. Book by Fred de Gressac; lyrics by B. G. DeSylva. 1922. Published by T. B. Harms, New York.

Dream Girl. Libretto by Rida Johnson Young. 1924. Published by T. B. Harms, New York.

Vaudeville Sketches

Miss Camille. Book by G. S. Hobart. 1908. Published by Witmark, New York.

Songbirds. Book by G. S. Hobart. 1910. Published by Witmark, New York.

APPENDIX

Incidental Music to Stage Productions

Cinderella Man, by Edward Childs Carpenter. 1905. Published by
Witmark, New York.

The Century Girl. Lyrics by Henry Blossom. 1916. Published by T. B.
Harms, New York. "Humpty Dumpty." "When Uncle Sam Is
Ruler of the Sea." "Romping Redheads." "You Belong to Me."

Ziegfeld Follies of 1917. Lyrics by Gene Buck. 1917. Published by
T. B. Harms, New York. "Can't You Hear Your Country Calling?"

Ziegfeld Follies of 1920. Lyrics by Gene Buck. 1920. Published by
T. B. Harms, New York. "When the Right One Comes Along."
"Love Boat."

Ziegfeld Follies of 1921. Lyrics by Gene Buck. 1921. Published by
T. B. Harms, New York. "In Khoressan." "Legend of the Golden
Tree." "Princess of My Dreams."

Ziegfeld Follies of 1922. Lyrics by Gene Buck. 1922. Published by
T. B. Harms. "Weaving My Dreams."

Ziegfeld Follies of 1923. Lyrics by Gene Buck. 1923. Published by
T. B. Harms, New York. "I'd Love to Waltz Through Life with
You." "Lady of the Lantern." "Old Fashioned Garden of Mine."

The Willow Plate. Five numbers from "A Chinese Shadowgraph,"
marionette play by Tony Sarg. For piano. 1924. Published by
T. B. Harms, New York.

INDEX

(For Herbert operettas and compositions see Appendix)

INDEX

INDEX

INDEX